DECISION MAKING
AND
PROBLEM SOLVING

Jerry R. McMurtry, Ph.D.
Doris D. Humphrey, Ph.D.
Career Solutions Training Group
Paoli, PA

VISIT US ON THE INTERNET
academic.cengage.com
www.cengage.com

SOUTH-WESTERN
CENGAGE Learning™

Australia • Brazil • Japan • Korea • Mexico • Singapore • Spain • United Kingdom • United States

Peter McBride: Business Unit Director
Eve Lewis: Team Leader
Laurie Wendell: Project Manager
Alan Biondi: Editor
Patricia Matthews Boies: Production Manager
Kathy Hampton: Manufacturing Coordinator
Mark Linton: Marketing Manager
Linda Wasserman: Marketing Coordinator

For permission to use material from this text or product,
contact us by web: www.cengage.com/permissions
Phone: 1-800-730-2214
Fax: 1-800-730-2215

Thanks to the following educators and trainers
who provided valuable assistance during the development of the QUICK SKILLS materials:

Robert W. Moses
Vice President for Planning and Program Development
Indian River Community College
Fort Pierce, Florida

Richard Winn
Director, Educational Projects
Heald Colleges
San Francisco, California

Debra Mills
Education-to-Careers/Tech Prep Director
Danville Area Community College
Danville, Illinois

Patrick Highland
Director of Vocational Education
Iowa City Community School District
Iowa City, Iowa

Julie Kibler
Business Teacher and Business Department Chairperson
Castle High School
Newburgh, Indiana

Dave Hyslop
External Liaison
Bowling Green State University
Bowling Green, Ohio

Dr. Doris Humphrey: Project Manager
Holly Johnson: Contributing Writer
Deborah Stuart: Production Editor
Pam Dooley: Typography

13 East Central Avenue, Paoli, PA 19301
Telephone: 1-888-299-2784 • FAX: (610) 993-8249
E-mail: cstg@bellatlantic.net • Website: www.careersolutionsgroup.com

CONTENTS

Every day you face problems that require decisions. This Quick Skills book provides strategies to help you make decisions and solve problems.

Your decision making starts when you get up in the morning and doesn't end until you go to sleep at night. Some decisions are so simple or automatic that they seem to require no thought. For example, when you come to a stop sign, you stop automatically for safety's sake.

Other decisions require time and a lot of thought. Should you change jobs? Should you buy a new or a used car? Decisions like these require you to gather information. This book tells you how to create a strategy and build a system for making decisions.

When solving problems, you must be able to think creatively, to come up with ideas that are fresh and new. You must also be able to look at both sides of an issue, evaluate all the information and think about how the information should be used. This book will help you with that process.

In Workshop 1 you will learn how to think differently and to demonstrate your creativity. Workshop 2 helps you develop strategies for critical thinking and describes how to apply them. By reading Workshop 3, you'll be able to make different types of decisions and gather information.

When you read Workshop 4, you'll learn to solve problems by using simple techniques. Then in Workshop 5, you'll decide how daily decisions are influenced by the big picture. Workshop 6 illustrates how change affects problem solving and provides methods for dealing with change.

In Workshop 7, you'll learn about team decision making and the advantages it offers. Finally, in Workshop 8, accountability for decision making is covered, giving you the tools you need to demonstrate responsibility as a decision maker.

> We are given one life, and the decision is ours whether to wait for circumstances to make up our mind, or whether to act, and in acting, to live.
>
> — Omar Bradley

Read the following statements to see where you stand on some of the issues required for problem solving and decision making. For each statement, circle the response that best fits you and your situation.

Total the number of times you circled Yes or Sometimes. If you circled a response only one or two times, this book can help you improve your problem-solving and decision-making skills.

1.	On the job I come up with new ideas to solve problems.	Y	N	Sometimes
2.	I try to avoid making decisions.	Y	N	Sometimes
3.	I have trouble solving problems.	Y	N	Sometimes
4.	I usually react to problems only when they become a crisis.	Y	N	Sometimes
5.	It is hard for me to look at both sides of an issue.	Y	N	Sometimes
6.	I don't like change.	Y	N	Sometimes
7.	Accountability is not a concern for me at work.	Y	N	Sometimes
8.	I have difficulty working on a team.	Y	N	Sometimes
9.	I try to stay away from people who suggest change.	Y	N	Sometimes
10.	I don't plan for solving problems or making decisions.	Y	N	Sometimes

Yolanda feels the tension and energy grow as her shipping staff at Caroline's Coats gears up for the upcoming fashion season. The goal is to ship as much merchandise as possible as fast as possible.

In each of the past four years, Yolanda's team has broken its prior year's record for the amount of merchandise shipped. Team members are so good at their work that it has created a problem with expectations. Her boss expects another increase in shipments this year. His motto is, "If you're not going faster, you're falling behind."

As Yolanda walks through the warehouse, she observes the new merchandise being hung on hangers in bins on the second floor. Getting items from upstairs to the loading dock has always been one of the most time-consuming tasks. "There must be a better way than carrying boxes down the steps," she thinks.

She pulls her team of seven together and lays out the problem, then she asks them to brainstorm a few ideas. "Think," she says, "about new ways to get the garments downstairs. Don't clutter your mind with how we've moved merchandise before. I want fresh ideas."

Georgette speaks up first, suggesting that they hang the coats on rolling carts. Yolanda agrees that carts speed up the process somewhat, but she's looking for an even greater time-saver. That's when Emanual offers his thoughts, "Why don't we install a pipe similar to a handrail between the first and second floors, then just slide the coats down the rail? We can have loaders at the top and catchers at the bottom."

"Yes! That's it," shouts Yolanda, as she makes a quick decision to try Emanual's suggestion. "The answer is so simple we overlooked it before."

> Some people have ideas. A few carry them into the world of action and make them happen.
>
> — Andrew Mercer

What's Inside

In these pages, you will learn to:

Connecting Decision Making and Problem Solving

Decision making and problem solving aided by critical thinking lead to great ideas, medical breakthroughs, and time-saving inventions. Without these three, there would be no space travel, no life-saving vaccines, no instant news from around the world, no cellular telephones, and no microwave ovens. You'd still be using carbon paper and a typewriter to make copies, and riding in a horse-drawn carriage instead of in a powerful engine-driven car.

Making decisions and solving problems takes courage, determination, and confidence. Too often we get stuck in a rut, continuing to do the same things over and over because it's more comfortable than developing new ways of thinking. Maybe you don't take the time to develop new ideas, or maybe you're afraid to try. In either case, you're losing out because you're not using the power of your brain to become more successful.

Decision making

Decisions are means, not ends. They help us achieve the answer to a question or the solution to a problem. Your decisions will vary depending on whether you make them as an individual or as a member of a group. Either type of decision making has its advantages and disadvantages. As an individual, you are influenced by your values and personality, but you're able to make decisions quickly without interference from others. When a group comes together to make a decision, many talents and skills focus on the same problem. The likelihood of a good decision increases, but group decision making usually takes longer. The group also shares the risk and the reward or blame.

Most of the time, one decision by itself won't lead to an answer; typically, you will go through a number of decision-making stages before solving your problem. If, for example, you consider moving to a larger apartment because the current one is too small, you'll have to decide whether you can afford the higher rent, who will help you move, how you'll get your furniture from one location to another, and whether you should take time off from work for the move.

> Mr. Podsnap had even acquired a peculiar flourish of his right arm in often clearing the world of its most difficult problems, by sweeping them behind him.
>
> — Charles Dickens, *Our Mutual Friend*

Decision-making techniques depend on the nature of the problem, time available, cost of individual strategies, and the mental skills of the decision makers. Your success will come from matching each problem with the appropriate decision-making techniques.

Personal values that you developed early in life play a role in every decision you make. If your parents treasured nature and objected to environmental tampering when you were a child, as an employee of a waste management company you will make choices that will be influenced by your background.

Whether you're an introvert or an extrovert, intuitive or structured, sensitive or objective shadows your decisions. Extroverts get their ideas out, even when other ideas may be more productive and profitable, because extroverts speak up. Introverts with good ideas frequently keep them hidden. Managers who are "soft-hearted" often make decisions that are detrimental to the company because they are influenced by the concerns of individuals and neglect the company's goals. As you make decisions, be aware of personal characteristics that influence your decision making.

Problem solving

A problem is a question looking for an answer. It's a straightforward process that requires (1) knowledge, (2) a few simple rules, and (3) practice.

♦ *Knowledge.* Your decision-making knowledge can be old, something you acquired in childhood, or new, encountered for the first time. It can come from daily observations or advanced study of specialized subjects.
♦ *Simple rules.* Establish where to start and what to do next. Then follow a problem solving plan.
♦ *Practice.* You don't become an expert at anything without practice. Consider how you learned to play baseball or golf, sing, dance, write, or use the computer.

The biggest decision-making challenge is to identify the real problem. If the problem is incorrectly identified, any decisions you make are directed toward solving the wrong problem. You may be considering a new apartment because you lack space; however, the problem may be that you don't utilize your current space well. Do you need to rearrange furniture, closets, and drawers to provide room for your things? Or is space an excuse to move because you're tired of the place you're in and need new scenery? There's nothing wrong with a change of scenery, but it is a different problem that has nothing to do with space. The five-step plan below will help you solve problems.

Problem solvers sometimes are surrounded by naysayers—people who don't like change and who reject most new ideas. If you run into any of these obstacle lovers, evaluate their concerns; and, if you still believe you are right, continue with your thinking. Have you heard these comments before?

"We can't do it that way."
"We've always done it this way."
"If it's not broken, don't fix it."
"Things are fine just the way they are."
"Nobody's paying me to think."
"You're just making more work for yourself."

Critical thinking

Critical thinking means looking at things in different ways. You can learn to think critically just as you can learn to write, make speeches, or become an engineer.

Look around you, and you'll see people who had ideas and developed them. Here are a few well-known examples.

♦ One person made a jacket out of old plastic soda pop bottles. Whether this was a good or bad idea is unclear, but the idea was different. Imagine staring at a pile of soda bottles and seeing a jacket.

Five-Step Problem-Solving Plan

Step 1: Collect information	Learn everything you can about the problem. "Airline passengers are becoming angry because overhead baggage space is too limited."
Step 2: Analyze the problem	Look at what is needed. • Add more baggage space • Limit the number of bags allowed per passenger • Redesign the existing space
Step 3: Summarize what you learn	"Three options are available for handling overhead baggage."
Step 4: Make a decision	Limit the number of bags allowed per passenger.
Step 5: Take action	Establish and enforce a two bags per passenger rule.

- The fireplace logs that you buy at the supermarket were, at one time, just sawdust. Today, they warm your house because a sawmill worker looked at a pile of sawdust and saw pressed fireplace logs.
- The inventor of Post-It™ notes stumbled upon the idea of small sticky notes while looking for a glue to be used in another way.
- Steve Jobs, a young college dropout, saw the computer of the future and built it in his garage. He's one of today's most famous thinkers.

When you explore a situation, think about a problem, or reach a conclusion that can be justified, you're thinking critically. Just think back over your day so far and you probably can make a list of problems you've solved just to get to this point. You may have encountered a traffic jam and sought an alternate route to work, or, if the clothes you planned to wear needed pressing, you probably chose something different. When you drove into the parking lot, perhaps you dropped your passenger off at the door so she wouldn't be late to work; or when a member of your team was delayed because of an appointment, you may have changed the time for today's meeting. In each of these instances, you thought about a variety of options and chose an answer based on your judgment and experience.

> " A hunch is an idea trying to tell you something. "
>
> — Frank Capra

Check Your Thinking

Do you look for new solutions or is your thinking tied to what you know from the past? Try the exercise below to determine whether you're an innovative thinker. Connect the nine dots with a single line without lifting your pencil off the paper. The answer can be found on page 10.

Taking a Chance

Innovative problem solving requires risk, and some people don't look for new and creative ideas because they're afraid. They take the path of least resistance because it's nonthreatening. Have you ever had a great work idea that you didn't submit to your supervisor because you were afraid of being humiliated if it was rejected?

Risk occurs when the decision maker has some information that makes an idea or plan seem worthy, but not enough information to guarantee results. Every time a bungee jumper goes off a bridge, a passenger enters a car or airplane, or an investor puts money in the stock market, risk is an element of the experience. Our background, intuition, and intelligence tell us how much risk to take; sometimes we decide the risk is too great.

Personality is an important factor in risk-taking. According to the Myers-Briggs Type Indicator, Perceptive or "P" personalities demonstrate a propensity for risk-taking, but the Judgmental, or "J" personalities, avoid risks and tend to make decisions based on the certainty of the outcome. They're the ones who say, "I'll get back to you later on that."

Female managers tend to take greater risks than male managers, according to Marcia A. Brodsky in her article "Successful Female Corporate Managers and Entrepreneurs" in the September 1993 issue of *Group & Organization Management*. Demographics support her conclusions, as female-owned businesses are the fastest growing segment of the economy, currently being founded at five times the rate of male-owned businesses.

Risk-averse employees appear to feel more comfortable in group decision-making activities where they share the risk. If you resist offering new ideas because of risk and you don't mind sharing credit, discuss your thoughts with co-workers. You're sure to find one who will advance your idea to the next level.

Not all ideas are worth their risk; that's why your supervisor doesn't accept all of yours. Suppose, for example, you can prove to your employer that the company will save tens of thousands of dollars if it closes for two weeks during the summer and forces all employees to take vacation at the same time. While the idea may have some merit, the risk of angering employees or customers by changing the schedule may be too high.

Suggestion boxes are placed at convenient places throughout companies all over the world so employees can anonymously offer their ideas. The suggestion box itself came into being because someone thought creatively about how to reduce the risk of being responsible for a bad idea.

> **Nothing ventured, nothing gained.**
>
> — Anonymous

ACTIVITY 1.2

Too Risky?

How risk-averse are you? Put yourself in the situations below, then mark Yes or No to express whether you would be willing to take the risk.

Risk Situation	I Would Take the Risk	
	Yes	**No**
1. A retired minister with an excellent pension, a young family, and a working wife considers whether to open a day care center with his retirement funds.	❑	❑
2. A small, growing business needs additional staff, but the owner can't guarantee that the business will continue to grow at the same rate.	❑	❑
3. A doctor who was once sued for medical malpractice believes he should perform a controversial procedure on his patient.	❑	❑
4. A science assistant sees a problem with the new antibiotic his team is developing and believes he should tell his supervisor, but his supervisor doesn't like anything to slow down the research project.	❑	❑
5. A young public relations assistant wants to pitch a story about her boss to a leading magazine, but she's afraid she'll be rejected because of her inexperience.	❑	❑
6. A software customer service representative sees a way to offer clients better service. She knows her company would want to hear it, but she doesn't like attention and she will be asked to make a short speech at the next staff meeting if her idea is accepted.	❑	❑
7. A consultant needs to tell her client that his son who works for the company is causing trouble among other employees, but the client has a history of "shooting the messenger."	❑	❑
8. A factory worker has thought of a way to get the production line moving faster, but he's not used to offering ideas.	❑	❑

If you answered No to more than five situations, you don't like risk. If you answered Yes to more than five situations, you're not afraid of risk.

Answer to Activity 1.1

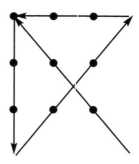

My Turn

Take a look back over the past several weeks at some of the decisions you've made. Choose one decision or problem that you might think differently about if it came up today and write a brief description of the decision on the first three lines below. Beneath those lines, write your new ideas about the decision or problem. Following that, write the risks involved in implementing your new ideas and state whether the risks are worth taking. If the risks are worth taking, describe the potential impact on your organization and on you.

The decision I made: _____

_____

_____

My new ideas today: _____

_____

_____

The risks to me of my new ideas: _____

_____

_____

The risks to my organization of my new ideas: _____

_____

_____

_____

Are the risks worth taking, to me? _____ to my organization? _____

What is the potential impact of my new thinking

on me? _____

_____

_____

on my organization? _____

_____

_____

_____

The Sacred Cow Problem

Organization rules may not support critical thinking, even when the company purports to encourage creativity. Some of these rules are formal and stated in company policy and others have been allowed to grow informally. Either can impact your creativity.

Think about the Olympics. What if there were rules that stated how fast you could go in track or Alpine skiing or how high you could jump in field events? Do you think the competitors would try harder? Of course not. The same is true when limits are placed on thinkers within an organization.

Sometimes organizations limit creative thinking without knowing what they're doing. When this occurs, you need to evaluate the situation.

> **Imagination is more important than knowledge.**
>
> — Albert Einstein

Learn whether anyone cares that an old obstacle is still around; and if not, ask your supervisor to get rid of the rule. One word of warning: Some rules that don't make sense to you may be very important to the organization, so challenge carefully.

Innovators Deal with Change

The creative people in an organization usually are known to most employees. They're the ones who say:

"I discovered . . . "
"I found a way around . . . "
"I developed a program for . . . "
"I motivated my employees to . . . "

Ideas actually come from anyone at any time, but they usually appear from people who are flexible, who can adapt to new ways, and who work well with change. Roger Van Oech, a creative thinking expert, says there are two good reasons for creative thinking: (1) the need for change and (2) the life span of ideas.

The need for change

Change is the only constant in life. Think about the changes in the past few years in your job, your personal life, or your education. Your life, most likely, has taken unexpected twists and turns. Then think about the revolution in computer software in just the past few months. If you're using software that's over a year old, it's probably outdated.

Life span of ideas

Ideas eventually die or become useless. When an idea occurs, you must jump on it quickly, run with it, and then come up with a new one. Being creative is just like exercising. You have to keep doing it, or the process doesn't work.

GETTING CONNECTED

You will find many Web sites devoted to creative thinking, critical thinking, and problem solving. Log on to the Internet and try entering the phrase "creative thinking" or "thinking outside the box" in an on-line search engine and see what you discover.

Here is one site to get you started:

http://www.ozemail.com.au/~caveman/Creative/index2.html

WORKSHOP WRAP-UP

- Making decisions and solving problems requires courage, determination, and confidence.
- New ideas come from thinking differently.
- A problem is a question looking for an answer.
- Some organizations' rules detract from creative thinking.
- Anyone can be creative; it just takes practice.

2 WORKSHOP

Eight months have passed since Gus, the plant manager at Ski Heights Manufacturing, first heard the roar of the new high-temperature press. He can still feel the excitement he felt the first time he watched layers of fiberglass and wood enter the press the first time for the laminating process. He was one of a team that traveled to Europe to evaluate the machine and recommend its use in the United States. When he first saw the skies come off the press, he knew that soon he would see skiers sliding down the nearby hills on the very skis that he was watching take form.

Now his mood is somber as his boss alerts him that the skis are delaminating after only a short time on the slopes. She tells Gus that he has four weeks to find out why and to fix the problem, or the factory will have to close and 146 people will lose their jobs.

Gus calls in his top craftspeople and explains the problem, then he sends them off to examine the returned skis, evaluate the equipment, and study the entire laminating process.

Two weeks later when he calls the team together, they don't have answers but they have more questions. Gus lists all their questions and comments on a flip chart, then they match the thoughts that seem to connect. A pattern relating to weather begins to emerge. Not yet sure what the problem is, the team goes back to work, eliminating all the suggestions that are not related to weather.

They soon realize that the factory in Europe using the same machine and process is located high in the Alps where the air is dry, while their factory is on the coast, where moisture keeps the layers from holding together. Once they figure out the problem, the solution is easy. Gus orders dehumidifying machines and the factory goes into full production within a week.

What's Inside

In these pages, you will learn to:

> Discovery consists of seeing what everybody has seen and thinking what nobody has thought.
>
> — Albert von Szent-Gyorgyi

The Process of Critical Thinking

The development of critical thinkers has gained priority attention at all educational levels, from elementary schools through colleges..

Critical thinking is creative thinking combined with intense questioning. It is well-founded, structured, and reinforced thinking that leads to good judgment, which in turn leads to wisdom.

It involves (1) exploring a situation, question, or problem, (2) generating a conclusion that uses all the available information, and (3) justifying the conclusion by making logical arguments.

Critical thinking is not what you hear on the radio, TV, or Internet; nor is it someone's opinion or an emotional response to a question. Opinions are not necessarily knowledge, and emotional responses certainly are not knowledge. For ordinary thinking to become critical thinking, it must rely upon criteria.

Ordinary Thinking	Critical Thinking
Guessing	Estimating
Preferring	Evaluating
Grouping	Classifying
Believing	Assuming
Inferring	Inferring logically
Associating concepts	Grasping principles
Noting relationships	Noting relationship among other relationships
Supposing	Hypothesizing
Offering opinions without reasons	Offering opinions with reasons
Making judgments without criteria	Making judgments with criteria

Several criteria that you can use as you develop your critical-thinking skills are shown below:

- Standards
- Laws, by-laws, rules, regulations
- Conventions, norms
- Principles, assumptions, definitions
- Ideals, goals, objectives
- Tests, credentials, codes of ethics
- Methods, procedures, policies

Creative thinkers break a problem down into its smallest parts and look at all the connections, including the context or situation in which the problem exists, then recombine the smaller parts into bigger parts that connect. This step of locating connections or new associations among seemingly unrelated ideas is the central point of critical thinking.

Gus broke the lamination problem into its smallest parts by first determining that the machine was in order and that raw materials met specifications. His team then questioned all other possible reasons the skis could be imperfect and compared their process with the process in Europe. When the only remaining

difference seemed to be the climates where the two factories were located, they made the connection between high humidity and delamination.

In his book *Cracking Creativity*, published by Ten Speed Press, Michael Michalko describes ways to break items down and re-form them into combinations that lead to reasonable conclusions.

Combining random objects

If you want to invent a product or service for your company, think of 20 objects at random that are related to the business and write them down, 10 in the left column and 10 in the right column. Pick one from the left and one from the right to form a promising new product or service. The following list of random objects needed by homebound patients and the people associated with homebound care was developed by a team of nurses whose supervisor wants to expand the company's offerings.

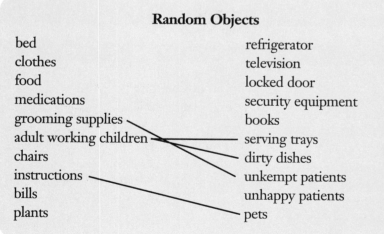

Random Objects

bed	refrigerator
clothes	television
food	locked door
medications	security equipment
grooming supplies	books
adult working children	serving trays
chairs	dirty dishes
instructions	unkempt patients
bills	unhappy patients
plants	pets

After making the four connections between the columns, the nurses saw the following ideas for expanded services in their random objects list. You may be able to make other connections for them.

- Combining adult working children with serving trays and dirty dishes suggests the needs for housecleaning services.
- Combining instructions with pets yields the need for walking.
- Combining food with refrigerators suggests the need for grocery shopping.
- Combining grooming supplies with unkempt patients shows promise for personal grooming assistance.

Combining unrelated fields

Michalko also suggests combining attributes of different subjects as a quick way to develop ideas. In the following example, a public relations assistant was asked to develop a brochure about the new services being offered by city government. She listed city services in the left column and randomly chose entertainment industry services for the right column. Then she made combinations that gave her ideas for the copy to be used in her brochure. You may be able to make other combinations for her.

- By combining libraries with relaxation, she can promote the city's libraries as a place to go for quiet time.
- By combining civic center facilities with concerts, she can describe how the city provides space for the shows that come to town.
- By combining taxi coordination with concerts, she can describe the efficient taxi service on big concert nights.

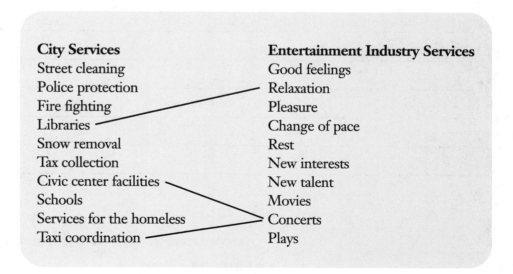

City Services	Entertainment Industry Services
Street cleaning	Good feelings
Police protection	Relaxation
Fire fighting	Pleasure
Libraries	Change of pace
Snow removal	Rest
Tax collection	New interests
Civic center facilities	New talent
Schools	Movies
Services for the homeless	Concerts
Taxi coordination	Plays

You Combine

Try developing random object combinations based on your work or the work you would like to do. Respond according to your own work or imagine that you work for a software company, a steel mill, a television station, or some other type of business or agency. In the left column, list 10 objects you would likely see as you walk down the halls and in the right column list 10 more objects. Pick one from the left and one from the right to combine. Describe the combinations they form that suggest a new invention or a new service.

Random Object Combinations from My Work

1.   11.

2.   12.

3.   13.

4.   14.

5.   15.

6.   16.

7.   17.

8.   18.

9.   19.

10.   20.

Combinations

• _____

_____

• _____

_____

_____

• _____

_____

> " Learning to think critically is one of the most significant activities of adult life. "
>
> — Stephen Brookfield

Techniques of Critical Thinking

Critical thinkers begin solving problems by exploring a situation, question, or problem, using a variety of techniques. By practicing the few simple techniques described below, you can become an excellent critical thinker.

Ask questions (What? When? Why? How?)
"You said you believe the trees in your yard are dying? As a landscaping company, we can help you. When did you notice the problem? What brought it to your attention? Have you seen spiders or other insects in the trees? Do you use chemicals on your lawn? When is a convenient time for our tree consultant to come look at the trees?"

Make checklists
"Here's what I will do to get my story ready for tomorrow morning's newspaper."
✓ Research the archives about voting patterns in the community.
✓ Interview people on the street about their choice of candidates.
✓ Take a photographer along to make pictures.
✓ Write the copy.
✓ Give a rough draft chart of the candidates' strengths and weaknesses to the graphic artist by 5 p.m.
✓ Make the 8 p.m. production deadline.

Brainstorm
"Let's think of every idea we can to increase sales for next quarter. I'm going to write all of our ideas on this chart paper; then at the end, we'll decide together which ones are best. Remember, during this brainstorming exercise, there are no bad ideas, so I want to hear everything that comes to your mind. It's very important for you to be respectful of others' contributions during brainstorming. Don't make any judgments about their ideas."

Imitate
"Once before we had all our elderly guests dressed, fed, and ready before 9 a.m. for their day trip, but lately it's been difficult to have everyone ready on time. Let's try to remember what we did before and do the same thing again."

Storyboard
"You describe how you think we should solve this problem, and I will draw some rough draft pictures in sequence. We can shift them around later to come up with better ideas."

Debate
"I appreciate your position, but here's my opinion. I believe you are wrong about the reasons that child abuse has increased. If you look at the statistics, you'll see . . ."

Role play	"I'll play the manager in this dispute, and you play the employee. As conflict resolution specialists, let's try to get inside their heads to understand why they have so many confrontations."
Reverse roles	"As human resources officer here at the company, I'd like to help you understand why your manager is so demanding about deadlines. Think of yourself as the manager for a few moments. How would you handle the urgency of a deadline?"
Explain to another person	"The first thing you do is establish the menu, then you order the supplies and ingredients. Start the salads after that."

ACTIVITY 2.2

What's the Best Technique?

Read each of the cases below and list the technique from the table above that you believe would be most helpful in solving the problem.

Case 1

A small regional soup company wishes to begin marketing its mushroom soup. It now sells the soup only to restaurants, where it is used to flavor other dishes. The soup is more expensive than other store brands because of its heavier stock and larger mushrooms. Your marketing team has been asked to develop a sales strategy.

Critical-Thinking Strategy_____

Case 2

A petroleum company's business offices are in one location about 20 miles from the oil tanks and trucks. The president, who describes himself as a hands-on manager, considers buying a larger building and combining the two locations. He asks you and your colleague to make recommendations.

Critical-Thinking Strategy_____

Case 3

A large bank has just purchased 14 smaller branches within a 100-mile radius. Some positions will be eliminated in the branches, but the bank wants to cushion the blow as much as possible. You and your human resources team are asked to develop a severance plan for the people who will lose their jobs.

Critical-Thinking Strategy_____

Case 4

Your company faces some difficult decisions about whether to take a loan and increase revenues quickly or grow slowly without a loan.

Critical-Thinking Strategy_____

Case 5

The nursery school children sometimes misbehave on their field trips. As lead teacher, you're asked for a plan for controlling them on the next trip.

Critical-Thinking Strategy_____

Case 6

In your job as copywriter, you work with an artist to produce public relations brochures. The two of you have been asked to develop a new brochure for the company's 20th birthday.

Critical-Thinking Strategy_____

Case 7

In your job as contract coordinator, your boss has asked you to warn a subcontractor that he will lose your account if he continues to miss deadlines.

Critical-Thinking Strategy_____

Case 8

You have been asked to develop a training plan for new hires in the customer service department of a discount store.

Critical-Thinking Strategy_____

> " Anyone can look for fashion in a boutique or history in a museum. The creative person looks for history in a hardware store and fashion in an airport. "
>
> — Robert Wieder

Sometimes the answer you're seeking through critical thinking will take days, weeks, months, or years to discover, and sometimes it will be right in front of your eyes. Several mental processes, strategies, and representations can help you solve problems, make decisions, and learn new concepts. Review the table below for ideas and examples.

Prioritize	"Before I can decide what's wrong with this car, the customer needs to tell me why he brought it in for repair; then I will listen to the noises the car makes, check a few hoses, and do computer diagnostics."
Identify purpose in	"This annual report describes why the company did so well this year and why I should continue to invest my money in the company."
Determine consequences	"If I miss work tomorrow, I may get in trouble."
Determine effects	"If a hurricane hits, I'll have to hire extra people quickly to work in my construction business."
Identify bias	"The reason this report on health focuses on dieting rather than exercise is that the research was funded by a company specializing in weight loss."
Identify assumptions	"I should hire extra employees for the holidays because the store will be busier than usual."
Draw conclusions	"According to this map, if I turn right at the next traffic light, I will be on the street where I am to deliver this package."
Make contrasts and comparisons	"These two fabric samples are similar; however, the colors are stronger in one than the other."
Synthesize	"From everything I've read and been told, the most important task for me as supervisor of the paramedic crew is to make sure we're properly staffed for this upcoming ice storm."
Develop and test hypotheses	"As principal of this school, I believe some of our elementary school students do poor work in the classroom because they don't eat breakfast. We will give students a snack each morning during the next few weeks, then compare their scores at the end of the grading period with their scores from the preceding grading period."
Critique	"The layout of the brochure is nice; however, the copy is unclear, and the people in the pictures don't match the age group of our market."
Summarize	"After listening to each of you talk, I think it's clear that our department is efficient but understaffed."

Which Strategies Are Best?

Using the chart on the previous page, list the mental processes, strategies, or representations from the table that would be most useful for each of the following problem-solving situations.

Problem	Useful Aid
1. I have two days to do many projects.	_____
2. The customer who wrote this obviously is angry.	_____
3. I'd like to put this report off for another day.	_____
4. I wonder what this report is about.	_____
5. The training manual doesn't seem complete.	_____
6. Why was Lyme Disease so prevalent last year?	_____

Jane: They are asking for answers for both of these activities. Pam

What Is Useful?

A manufacturer's representative has identified new markets for her inexpensive, trendy costume jewelry. Review and prioritize her list from 1 to 7. Use 1 for people who should be easy to sell to and 7 for those people on whom she should not waste her time. Explain the reason for each priority.

Possible Customers	Priority Order	Reason for This Priority
High-income customers	_____	_____
Event or partygoers	_____	_____
Low-salaried customers	_____	_____
Teenagers	_____	_____
Elderly customers	_____	_____
Men buying gifts for women	_____	_____
Children buying gifts for parents	_____	_____

GETTING CONNECTED

You can find many Web sites devoted to critical thinking. Log on to the Internet and try entering the phrase "critical thinking" into an on-line search engine and see what you discover.

Here is one site that contains an exercise in critical thinking skills.

http://www.abacon.com/baron/critical.html

> " Knowledge is the door;
> thinking is the key. "
>
> — B. G. Trickett

WORKSHOP WRAP-UP

- Critical thinking is a national priority.
- Critical thinking is creative thinking combined with intense questioning.
- For ordinary thinking to become critical thinking, it must rely on criteria.
- Critical thinking breaks a problem down into its smallest parts then re-forms the parts into other combinations.
- Locating connections among seemingly unrelated ideas is the central point of critical thinking.

Heading up manufacturing at Northeastern Steel had been Amy's dream since she came to work eight years ago; so when Eric retired last spring, she applied for his job. The only female competing with six men in a traditional male business took courage, but she knew that she had a good education, the right experience, and a take-charge attitude.

Now, reading over the company's largest order ever, one that will keep the plant busy for two years, she knows she's facing some tough decisions. This multi-million-dollar contract requires a two-fold production increase and 25 additional people. In a healthy steel industry economy like today's, finding even one new hire in her small town challenges her ingenuity.

Amy's boss, Ben, the plant manager, presses her daily for a hiring plan. He suggests going with a part-time staff, but her last experience with part-timers left her wringing her hands and saying, "Never again."

Amy's hiring dilemma nags at her; and just to get a good night's sleep, she has to make a decision soon. Whom does she bring in? How does she locate them? Will they all be new? Should she reassign people from the plant on the West coast? If she does, will the cost of moving entire families to the Northeast for two years cut into profits too heavily? How does she quickly get all the information she needs before making a decision?

As she thinks through her options, Amy knows her final decision will have an enormous impact on many people and on the company. The pressure is intense.

> To live is to make decisions, and to make decisions is to grow intellectually.
>
> — J. P. Guilford

What's Inside

In these pages, you will learn to:

Three Types of Decisions

Decisions can be categorized according to the amount of time available. For planning purposes in your work, you should think in terms of (1) long-range, (2) medium-range, and (3) short-range decisions. All decisions should be taken seriously because they build on one another.

Long-range decisions. These decisions take years to make; they are the most risky. *Should the company move to another city?*

Medium-range decisions. These decisions may occur within the next month or two. They are less risky and support your long-range decisions. *Should the current building lease be renewed for one year, two years, or five years?*

Short-range decisions. You make these every day. They support your medium-range decisions and usually aren't risky. *Should new letterhead showing the current address be reordered?*

Locating Information

Some decisions are easy. Which task to do first, what to order for lunch, when to begin compiling the monthly sales report, or where to purchase office supplies fall into the easy category because they're routine. You make these decisions without spending too much time considering the options. Other decisions are harder, especially when they impact the lives of co-workers and the profitability of the company.

To make any decision, you need information. Good information leads to good decisions. Amy's first step was to get information about sources for plant workers.

You can make decisions based on hunches and guessing, but the risk is greater when you do. The best decisions are carefully reasoned after all available information has been reviewed. Imagine making a decision on whether to purchase laser, ink-jet, or dot-matrix printers for your office without learning about their differences. Dot matrix printers are appealing if you base your decision solely on price. However, with additional information, you might decide that the appearance of the printed documents doesn't fit the image of your company.

> " Nothing is more difficult, and therefore more precious, than to be able to decide. "
>
> — Napoleon Bonaparte

Timing Our Decisions

Right now, several decisions await your action. In the spaces below, list one long-range decision related to your work or school and two medium-range and short-range decisions that support the long-term decision. Think carefully about your long-range decision, because it will influence many of your actions in the next days, weeks, and months.

My long-range decision: _____

Medium-range decisions that support my long-range decision:

1. _____

_____

_____

2. _____

_____

_____

Short-range decisions that support my medium-range and long-range decisions:

1. _____

_____

_____

2. _____

_____

_____

> " Out of clutter, find simplicity. From discord, find harmony. In the middle of difficulty lies opportunity. "
>
> — *Little Zen Companion*

See the problem in action

The best way to get information or collect data is to see the problem in action. You can do this by observing people, procedures, and equipment. You can also interview people. For example, if an ice cream store always has long lines of customers, observe what's happening behind the counter. Is the space adequate? Are enough servers available? Are their procedures efficient? Is the amount and type of equipment suitable for the job?

All people who will be influenced by the way a problem is solved should be included in information collection. For example, a store that is deciding what hours to open on Sunday needs to know how the hours will affect everyone from the janitorial staff to the accounting staff. Some of the people, procedures, and equipment to observe are listed below.

- *People to observe:* employees, customers, managers, visitors, suppliers, salespeople.
- *Procedures to observe:* steps involved, number of people involved at each step, type of records being kept, troubleshooting methods.
- *Equipment to observe:* machines, electrical devices, software programs

Read

Another way to collect information is to read or computer search publications from the trade or industry you work in. Some of these magazines from different industries are *Electrical World, Woodworker, Hairdressers Journal International,* and *The Professional Medical Assistant.* Trade publications often contain articles that troubleshoot problems. They also run stories about companies that are successful in solving a specific problem.

Procedure manuals are another important source of information. Air conditioning technicians and employees from other industries couldn't possibly know how to repair every brand, so they refer to manuals for help.

Other ideas

Information can be obtained in additional ways. Here are suggestions that may help you.

- Use an employee suggestion box, and give a cash award for good ideas.
- Provide a courtesy card offering a gift to customers who make good suggestions.
- Send a follow-up letter to customers asking for opinions.
- Ask teams of employees or managers to study a problem and make recommendations.

Sources of Information

✓ General books	✓ Opinion surveys
✓ Technical manuals	✓ Personal interviews
✓ Newspapers	✓ Observation of people
✓ Magazines	✓ Seminars and workshops
✓ Internet	✓ Employee suggestion box
✓ Software programs	

Gathering Information

What sources of information might the decision makers use in each of the situations described below?

Situation	Information Sources

1. Your fashion designer boss is deciding what types of clothes to design for the winter season next year. He asks you to do some research that will help him with his decisions.

_____
_____
_____

2. As a computer numerical control (CNC) machine operator who wants to be promoted to the next level, you see the need for additional education.

_____
_____

3. In your work as a motivational speaker, you incorporate jokes about national trends into your talks. You're currently planning a big presentation for a car manufacturer's convention.

_____
_____
_____

4. As a placement specialist with a temporary personnel placement firm, you match personnel with temporary jobs. More jobs exist than people to fill them, and you're looking for ways to attract potential workers.

_____
_____
_____

5. Arranging for your company's exhibit at big conventions requires you to make decisions about the design of the exhibits, amount of space to rent, type of marketing materials to give away, and many similar small details.

_____
_____
_____

6. Your boss plans to travel to Hong Kong for a conference and has asked you to plan the trip. You'll need to coordinate time zone differences for airline travel, obtain the services of Chinese interpreters, and decide which Hong Kong hotels to use.

_____
_____
_____

> " Some people, however long their experience
> or strong their intellect, are temperamentally
> incapable of reaching firm decisions. "
>
> — James Callaghan

Using a T-chart

A T-chart is a simple graphic that shows the alternatives to consider when you need to make a decision. It forces decision makers to look at pros and cons, positives and negatives, and promotes decision making based on facts.

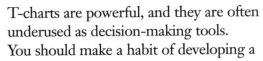

By keeping you focused on your decision, a T-chart reduces your risk of making an ill-informed decision based on too few facts.

T-charts are powerful, and they are often underused as decision-making tools. You should make a habit of developing a T-chart for all your important decisions.

The T-chart below was constructed by a decision maker who needs to decide whether to hire college students for a six-month research project.

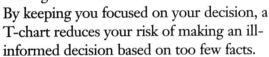

T-chart

College Student Pros
- Available now
- Low daily pay rate
- Long-term employment not needed
- No employment benefits required

College Student Cons
- Training required
- Competing priorities between work and school
- Schedule conflicts
- Lack of loyalty common to temporary workers.

> 66 Indecision and delays are the parents of failure. 99
>
> — George Canning

Your T-Chart

Take some time to think about an upcoming important decision you need to make, then construct a T-chart of the positives and negatives associated with the decision.

Decision I need to make: _____

_____

Pros	Cons
_____	_____
_____	_____
_____	_____
_____	_____
_____	_____
_____	_____
_____	_____
_____	_____

Constructing a Decision Value Chart

Another way to make sound decisions is by using a Decision Value Chart. With this technique, a decision maker lists in column one the criteria the decision must meet and in column two the points assigned to the criteria based on their importance. Alternative decisions are listed in additional columns and points are given to each alternative according to how fully it meets the criteria. A scale of 1 to 5 or 1 to 10 or any other range that makes sense can be used.

In the example below, the decision maker is a travel agent who has been asked to organize a corporate planning retreat for the company's five top officers.

Excitement, relaxation, scenery, and ease of access are the criteria against which each location will be measured. Review the example to see how a Decision Value Chart works.

Once all the choices have been assigned points, the points are totaled and the choice with the highest total is selected. You can see that, overall, the trip to Jamaica is the winner, with staying home coming in as the loser. The fishing trip is in second place and next year it might win if the important measures change.

A Decision Value Chart helps you keep track of the many pieces of information that go into every decision. You set the criteria and decide on the points and alternatives. If you are honest with yourself and have a complete set of measures, this tool is excellent.

Decision Value Chart

Criteria	Possible Points	Jamaica	Canada Fishing	Staying Home
Excitement	25	15	25	5
Relaxation	25	25	20	20
Scenery	25	25	25	0
Ease of access	25	20	10	25
Total points	100	85	80	50

> In any moment of decision, the best thing you can do is the right thing, the next best thing is the wrong thing, and the worse thing you can do is nothing.
>
> — Theodore Roosevelt

My Decision Value Chart

Construct a Decision Value Chart to help you with the decision you listed in Activity 3.3. Begin by jotting down the criteria points and alternatives related to your decision. Remember that point values don't have to be equal. For an on-the-job decision, you might have higher values on criteria that relate to the culture of the company or on measures that your boss favors. As long as you are honest and seek out good information, you can assign points that you feel are correct.

Criteria	Possible Points	Alternative	Alternative	Alternative
_____	_____	_____	_____	_____
_____	_____	_____	_____	_____
_____	_____	_____	_____	_____
_____	_____	_____	_____	_____
_____	_____	_____	_____	_____
_____	_____	_____	_____	_____
Total points	_____	_____	_____	_____

GETTING CONNECTED

Use this Web site to get more information about decision making and personality:

http://www.valdosta.edu/~whuitt/psy702/files/prbsmbti.html

Implementing Decisions

Once you have reached a decision, the job is half done. The next step is to implement the decision. It's important to note that failing to implement a decision is a decision in itself. People usually fail to implement because they are not completely sold on their choice. When this occurs, you need to go back to the beginning. Once a decision is made, it is time to move on. Don't dwell on your choice or worry about it.

You will always have decisions to make. They will be with you throughout your life. You can think of the decision-making process as a wheel with each spoke a part of the decision-making process.

From the wheel you can see that making decisions never stops. It is a process that gets easier the more you do it. Starting with small decisions sets you up and gives you practice for making bigger and more difficult decisions.

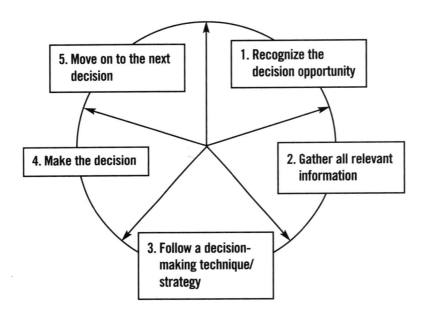

5. Move on to the next decision

1. Recognize the decision opportunity

4. Make the decision

2. Gather all relevant information

3. Follow a decision-making technique/strategy

WORKSHOP WRAP-UP

- Decisions can be characterized as long-range, medium-range, and short-range.
- Good information leads to good decisions.
- A T-chart is a graphic representation of positives and negatives.
- A Decision Value Chart is based on criteria and choices.

WORKSHOP

4

Daniel's firm of manufacturing reps has upgraded its computers for better tracking and billing of customers. As manager of a team of 30 invoice processing and customer service personnel, he has a few concerns about his employees' ability to jump from a manual tracking and billing system to one that is totally computerized. To prepare them, he asks the software vendors to provide three days' training.

When Daniel examines the invoice production report the first week following training, he discovers that the number of invoices processed is fewer than before. "What is the problem?" he wonders.

In a quick meeting with a few employees, Daniel learns that they aren't confident about using the system so he orders training manuals they can review when they have a question. The following week when he examines the production report again, he sees another drop. Daniel is confused. The software engineers provided training manuals full of diagrams, so lack of information shouldn't be the problem.

His first stop after seeing the report is at the processing center where he gets a first-hand look at what's going on. As he watches the billing staff, he realizes that they stop often to review the manuals—just what he expected. But, instead of spending a few minutes with the manuals, they're taking up to twenty or thirty minutes for reading, trying out, and rereading. Some ask their neighbors questions, which ties up two people.

When Daniel draws a small group of staff together to brainstorm the problem, he learns that the training, though helpful, was too much theory with too little practice and that the training manuals are confusing. The employees needed time to practice— to try the software out in different invoicing situations.

> Every decision is liberating, even if it leads to disaster. Otherwise, why do so many people walk upright and with open eyes into their misfortune?
>
> — Elias Canetti

What's Inside

Identify The Real Problem

According to the American Society for Training and Development and the U.S. Department of Labor, an organization's ability to achieve its goals depends on the problem-solving skills of its workforce. If your education did not include learning how to problem solve, developing this skill now is essential to your career growth and success.

In Workshop 3, you learned how to collect information—the first step in problem solving. The second step is to analyze and identify the problem. Daniel identified the invoicing problem as lack of training, but he didn't analyze the situation carefully enough to identify the full problem, which was the employees' limited computer knowledge.

Problem solving requires looking at a situation deeply. Like Daniel, people sometimes see symptoms as the problem and overlook the real problem. It's like thinking a fever is the illness when the fever is actually a symptom of an infection. Treating the fever will not cure the illness.

ACTIVITY 4.1

Elusive Problem

Chances are you have experienced work or school-related problems in the last few days. On the lines below, state the problem and the symptoms. Follow by writing your first diagnosis of the problem. Think further and decide whether you identified the real problem. If you didn't, write the real problem on the next line. An example is provided.

Example

Main problem:	*Copier jammed*
Symptom:	*Machine stopped*
First diagnosis of problem:	*Equipment problem*
Real problem:	*Wrong type of paper was used*

My problem

Main problem:	_____
Symptom:	_____
First diagnosis of problem:	_____
Real problem:	_____

Quick Skills

Summarize in Simple Terms

The third step in problem solving after locating information and analyzing the problem is summarizing what you learned. Your summary should describe the problem in simple, specific, brief, and well researched terms. List any negatives that need to be considered.

A typical summary statement of a customer problem is shown below.

Marsha and Ramon Gonzales ordered a wedding cake for their daughter's wedding. When Mrs. Gonzales picked up the cake, she discovered that the bride and groom on the top were not the ones she selected. A long-awaited, perfectly planned wedding is off to a bad start before the ceremony begins.

The problem occurred because the order taker had several customers and did not write the instructions immediately. When he did find time, he had forgotten exactly which bride and groom Mrs. Gonzales chose. Since they were all so similar, he wrote a description of the set he suspected she chose. This problem occurred because the order taker failed to complete the transaction at the time it occurred.

This is the second instance this month when one of our order takers confused a request. We need to confirm all details with the customers and have them sign the order form before it is given to the bakers.

Solve It

Once you summarize a problem, finding a solution can be easy or difficult. If for example, you determine that the company doesn't get orders out on time, the solution may be to hire extra help. If the problem doesn't have a readily apparent solution, you may need to go back to step one and research additional information, or you can utilize some of the critical thinking skills described in Workshop 2.

Asking other people to help is also worthwhile when facing a tough problem. You can't expect to know all the answers all the time, and asking for help is a sign of leadership. Brainstorming with a group of talented people works effectively. In brainstorming, the group focuses on a problem, comes up with as many interesting and unusual solutions as possible, and pushes these ideas as far as it can.

It's important to remember that no idea is bad or silly. By writing ideas on a chart, you can go back later and see what was said. Thinking as you talk, writing the thoughts down, and returning to them later lead to creative solutions that build on one another. You can brainstorm alone also. All it takes is some paper, a pencil and time to think.

One brainstorming technique is to generate 26 ideas, one for each letter of the alphabet. This method is demonstrated on the next page. In the example, the problem-solving team was trying to produce more products with the same number of employees.

Twenty-Six Letters

A Ask other departments for help.
B Bring new methods to the production process.
C Create a flexible schedule that allows for three shifts.
D Do an efficiency chart to determine whether time is wasted.
E Energize the staff with rewards.
F Ferret out the slackers.
G Gather supplies faster.
H Hunt for speedier equipment.
I Illustrate time-saving techniques on charts on the production department walls.
J Juggle priorities so that the most important work is completed first.
K Keep breaks to the allocated time.
L Load supplies on moving carts that workers can reach handily.
M Match fast and slow workers in teams.
N Notch pieces so they fit together easily.
O Open supply boxes before they hit the production room floor.
P Pick up the pace.
Q Query workers on time-saving techniques
R Reduce production time.
S Save the easiest work for last.
T Take staggered bathroom breaks
U Utilize management on the production floor during peak periods.
V Visit other company sites to see how they produce efficiently.
W Weed out the reasons for lost time.
X Execute production orders promptly.
Z Zip finished products into a bag instead of taping.

Try Brainstorming

Take any problem, perhaps the one from Activity 4.1, and try the 26-letter brainstorming method. State the problem, then write problem-solving possibilities that use 26 verbs, each beginning with a letter of the alphabet.

Twenty-Six Letter Method

A _____

B _____

C _____

D _____

E _____

F _____

G _____

H _____

I _____

J _____

K _____

L _____

M _____

N _____

O _____

P _____

Q _____

R _____

S _____

T _____

U _____

V _____

W _____

X _____

Y _____

Z _____

Make a Decision

The fourth step in problem solving is making a decision. Most problems can be solved in several ways, all of which may be good. You should develop two or three good solutions, then choose the one you believe is best in the situation. Doctors, for example, can prescribe several remedies for a sprained ankle, but they choose the one they think is best for each patient's situation.

Here are several points to consider when deciding on a solution.

♦ What is important to the company?

♦ What is important to the company's customers?

♦ What is important to me as the problem solver?

The example below shows how a bank applied these questions to its problem of extending hours to late afternoons and Saturdays.

9 a.m. - 3 p.m. Monday through Friday	The tellers and managers are able to count the money, balance their books, and leave by 5 p.m. if we close at 3:00. Overtime hours or subcontracted employees are not required.
9 a.m. - 3 p.m. Monday, Tuesday, and Wednesday 9 a.m. - 6 p.m. Thursday and Friday	Customers can come in after work two days a week. A limited number of tellers will be needed during the late hours, so overtime or outside help will not be needed. This schedule increases the payroll slightly.
9 a.m. - 3 p.m. Monday, Tuesday, Wednesday and Thursday; 9 a.m. - 6 p.m. Friday; 9 a.m.-noon, Saturday	Customers can come in after work one day a week or on Saturday morning. The bank may get new customers, however, outside help will be needed. They may be less dependable, and payroll will increase substantially.

> No idea is so outlandish that it should not be considered with a searching but at the same time steady eye.
>
> — Winston Churchill

Telephone Dilemma

The manager of a sports shoe store where you work is concerned because several customers have complained about delayed service, both when they call and come by in person. They are especially annoyed when they telephone because the phone sometimes goes unanswered for up to ten rings. You've learned through data collection and analysis that too few workers are on duty during peak hours, but to hire more employees will be costly for the store. How will you solve the problem? Form a team with three others to discuss the solution, then write your answers.

What is the problem?_____

_____

What is the solution?_____

_____

_____

_____

Take Action

Deciding to do something and doing it are two different things. At some point, you have to act, because there's no solution until you do.

Actions usually are easy after the decision to act is made. The list below describes a few actions that you will take to solve problems during your career.

Problem-Solving Actions

Complete a purchase order
Make a phone call
Write a letter
Develop a contract
Buy equipment
Rent larger space

Request a meeting
Visit a client
Make a claim
Complete a form
Reprimand a worker
Hire more employees

> Shelving hard decisions is the least ethical course of action.
>
> — Adrian Cadbury

Your Actions

List the actions you took after reaching a decision about how to solve a problem. Write the problem in column 1 and the action in column 2.

Problem

1. *Need to replace my computer.*

2.

3.

4.

5.

Action

Visited several computer stores.

The urgency with which you act depends on the priority of the problem. Think about the urgency of the accounting decisions discussed below.

A small accounting firm's owner knows the April 15 tax deadline is coming up in three months. He needs to make a decision quickly about how many accountants to hire for the tax season. Another small employer, a bicycle shop isn't so concerned about hiring its first full-time

accountant, although one is needed. This company owner may take a few weeks or months to make such an important decision.

After taking action, track your solution and evaluate whether you correctly solved the problem. If you need to adjust what you did and come up with a new solution, that's okay. You learn from each solution you implement. As you solve more and more problems, the process becomes easier.

> The significant problems we face cannot be solved at the same level of thinking we were at when we created them.
>
> — Albert Einstein

Adjust The Solution

Select a work-related problem that you encountered today and think about how you could have solved it differently. Relate the questions below from the Five-Part Problem-Solving Process to your problem.

The problem I solved: _____

_____

_____

1. Did I collect enough information? _____ Yes _____ No

If no, what additional information should I have obtained? _____

_____

2 _____Did I analyze the problem thoroughly? _____ Yes _____ No

If no, what did I overlook? _____

3. Is my summary of the problem shown at the top of this activity simple and complete? _____ Yes _____ No

If no, here's how I would rewrite the summary _____

_____

4. Was my solution appropriate? _____ Yes _____ No

If no, what better way could I have solved the problem? _____

_____

5. Were my actions appropriate? _____ Yes _____ No

If no, what actions would have been more appropriate? _____

_____

Advance your career

Organizations can't function without problem solving. Look for chances to solve problems and learn from each one you solve. As your skills grow, you will become more valuable to your employer and advance your opportunities for career growth. Practice the problem-solving process on your personal problems for additional skill building

GETTING CONNECTED

The Internet is full of sites that deal with problem solving. Try searching for "problem solving" by entering these words in a search engine after you log on. Try the site listed below to get started:

http://www.mindtools.com/page2.html

WORKSHOP WRAP-UP

- An organization's ability to achieve its goals depends on the problem-solving skills of the workforce.
- Problem-solving summaries should be simple, specific, brief, and well researched.
- Finding a solution can be easy or difficult.
- At some point, you must act.

or months, your friend Michael has asked you to take programming classes with him after work, so the two of you will be more knowledgeable when customers call with computer system problems. Your attitude from the beginning has been that customer support representatives, such as you and Michael, should let the company's programmers figure out what's wrong when a customer calls. As a young mother, you have big responsibilities at home, and you aren't paid enough to give up personal time to learn something that others can do.

"Amy," Michael says one morning, "I've registered for the new classes that start next month. If you don't take them now, you may not get another chance until next year."

You snap at him, "Michael, no way, I don't have time, and I don't need to know programming for this job. What I need is more money and less pressure."

Three weeks later, a memo announcing a new division of the company appears on your desk. Customer service representatives with moderate knowledge of computer programming may choose to work with their clients directly from home two days a week. You love the idea since you'll be able to stay home with your children.

You immediately rush to register for the classes Michael told you about. Even though the classes don't start for a week, they're full and eight people are ahead of you on the waiting list.

> Prediction is very difficult, especially of the future.
>
> — Neils Bohr

What's Inside

In these pages, you will learn to:

Seeing The Big Picture

Your problem solving value to an employee increases substantially when you are able to place current activities and events in the context of a bigger picture. As you look around at the most successful people, you'll recognize a few big thinkers. They're the ones whose minds are always working, who hear what a co-worker says and take it to a higher level, who connect current problems to future opportunities, who see potential dilemmas that may influence the future.

Amy focuses on daily problems and stresses. She allows personal concerns to influence her problem solving skills; and as a result, she lost an opportunity that she wanted.

Big thinkers apply their day-to-day activities to a larger picture. Their minds explore how what's happening today can help or hurt the future. While big thinkers have as many daily personal stresses as everyone else, they don't let them interfere with their decision-making ability. It's important to remember that the company pays you to make decisions in its best interest. What happens at home should stay at home.

By seeing the big picture, you can take action to curtail problems or to circumvent or delay them until you reach a desirable solution. While none of us can expect to predict the future accurately at all times, clues surround us. We often overlook the clues because we take a small view. We overlook events, subtleties, nuances, and trends that allow us to anticipate the future.

Recognizing clues is a skill. To some extent, it's intuitive and some people are better at it than others. Review the clues in the situations described below.

- A client who calls with complaints provides clues about poor service.
- Several malpractice lawsuits against a physician provides a warning to other patients.
- A supplier who consistently ships late provides clues about its level of dependability.
- An employee who speaks negatively about a supervisor or about the company provides clues of disloyalty.
- Products returned because of flaws suggest the production process needs evaluating.
- Continuing loss of sales quarter after quarter indicates a problem with the product or with the sales force.

> There is no future in any job. The future lies in the person who holds the job.
>
> — George Crane

A Hunt for Clues

Several situations are described in the left-hand column. Interpret the clues contained in each situation and, in the right-hand column, write how each potential problem can be solved.

Situation

How To Solve

1. A teacher receives several irate telephone calls from parents about one student's hostile behavior.

   The teacher should work with guidance counselors and the hostile student's parents to correct the problem or remove the student from the classroom.

2. A new employee finds things wrong with the company almost from the first day.

3. A toy company gets merchandise returned frequently.

4. A worker complains of chronic back pain and misses work often.

5. A package engineer's designs are frequently rejected.

6. A legal firm receives complaints of overbilling.

7. A dentist consistently loses dental assistants to larger practices.

8. A developer encounters hostility from home owners over a planned shopping center.

9. A toaster oven manufacturer is sued four times for burns customers receive when operating the oven.

10. A salesperson seems unable to close sales.

Proactive, Non-Active, and Reactive Thinking

Recognizing clues isn't enough—it's how you use the clues that counts. You may choose three approaches to problem solving: (1) proactive, (2) no action, or (3) reaction.

♦ A proactive problem solver creates the future based on information and critical thinking. The entire process of strategic planning is about being proactive. Most organizations today have developed a strategic plan so they will be able to mold and manipulate events to fit the future they desire.

Competition is intense, and individuals or companies who allow events to unfold without making contingency plans will enjoy limited success.

♦ A reactive problem solver waits until something happens, then responds. Reaction is the opposite extreme of proaction. In a reactive mode, you can't call the shots; you just try to stabilize events or circumstances after a crisis so they do the least harm. You react to a crisis without looking at how it influences the future.

♦ A no-action person is not a problem solver. This individual goes with the flow. In this state, you're just waiting. You're not reacting to a crisis nor looking to the future. No action often leads to reaction because circumstances sneak up when you aren't ready for them. Look at the chart below to better understand the differences between pro-action, no action, and reaction approaches to problem solving.

Problem-Solving Approaches

Proactive	Non-Active	Reactive
Anticipate change	Wait and see	Respond to change
Make changes happen	Wait and see	Resist change
Lead the way	Do nothing	Try to keep up
Think intuitively	Do nothing	Take events at face value
Be prepared	Do nothing	"Let sleeping does lie."
Think strategically	Do nothing	Think after the event occurs
See the big picture	Do nothing	"Take care of the little things and the big things will take care of themselves.

A Proactive Response

Read the case described below, interpret the clues, and write what you believe is the proactive response to the problem.

Case

A software producer who introduces a new program almost immediately gets requests from customers for information about the upgrade, including when will the upgrade be available? what are the new features? and how much will the upgrade cost? The software company hasn't anticipated the need for an upgrade so soon and expects resistance from the writers, producers, coordinators, and suppliers of the project who want to wait to see how the current product performs before developing an upgrade. The company's goal is to create its future by developing products the customers want.

1. Would you begin to develop the upgrade immediately?_____yes_____no

2. What are the potential problems that have to be considered? _____

_____

_____

_____

_____

_____

3   How would you proactively solve the problems you described in No. 2?

_____

_____

_____

_____

_____

_____

> " I hold that man is in the right who is most closely in league with the future. "
>
> — Henrik Ibsen

Taking Advantage of Trends

The one thing we know for sure is that we know nothing about the future. We have some good ideas about what might happen, but they're never a sure thing. A proactive problem solver studies trends and tries to stay ahead of the them. This type of thinker minimizes risk by getting the best information possible and learning from the experience of others.

A few good questions to ask if you want to be a proactive problem solver are listed below.

1. What are the trends in my industry?
2. Which trends impact the company or me personally?
3. How can I utilize the trends to my company's advantage and my personal advantage?
4. What problems will I encounter if I try to stay ahead of trends?
5. What can I do now to reduce problems later?

The trend toward weight and health consciousness has allowed proactive thinkers to provide a unique group of products and services. Here are a few:

Weight-loss clinics
Fat-free foods
Diet books
Exercise studios
Audio and videotapes
Support groups
Nutrition consultants
Weight camouflaging clothes

The aging population also created opportunities for proactive thinkers. Have you noticed any of these new products and services?

Assisted living centers
Adult day care centers
Senior citizens centers
Retirement communities
Home health care services
Recreation for older adults
Anti-aging products
Transportation services
Early bird dinner specials
Senior citizen pricing at movies

You have many sources for information about trends, including the Internet, newspapers, magazines, journals, books, and discussion groups.

> " Do not choose to be wrong for the sake of being different. "
>
> — Lord Samuel

Start At Work

Think about the industry that employs you or one you'd like to enter. Close your eyes and look into the future. What trends do you see that will affect this industry? Write a description of the trends in the spaces provided. As a proactive thinker, what problems or opportunities do you expect to result from these trends? Give one example of how you would solve each problem.

My industry:

_____

_____

Trend One:

_____

_____

Potential problem or opportunity:

_____

_____

My solution to the problem:

_____

_____

Trend Two:

_____

_____

Potential problem or opportunity:

_____

_____

My solution to the problem:

_____

_____

Taking the Risk

In an earlier workshop you learned about risk taking. Taking advantage of trends and becoming a proactive problem solver requires taking risk. Review the traits of a risk taker that are shown below for a reminder of whether you handle risk well.

Traits of a risk taker

✓ Stimulated by challenge
✓ Flexible
✓ Optimistic
✓ Excited by what's ahead
✓ Not afraid of criticism
✓ Removes obstacles to challenges
✓ Overcomes objections of nay-sayers
✓ Relies on good information

> " The best way to predict the future is to create it. "
>
> — Peter Drucker

Evaluate the Risk

Take some time to think about a problem that exists in your work. Perhaps it's lack of time during an average day to produce the high-quality work you want. Weigh the risks of doing your work differently and mark High, Medium, or Low to identify the level of risk. Examples are shown.

Situation	Risk Factor		
	High	**Medium**	**Low**
• Staying late on personal time to produce high quality products			X
• Reducing product quality during regular work hours	X		`
• Confronting a co-workers whose mistakes create problems in your work		X	
_____	_____	_____	_____
_____	_____	_____	_____
• Your Problem:			
_____	_____	_____	_____
_____	_____	_____	_____
_____	_____	_____	_____
_____	_____	_____	_____
_____	_____	_____	_____
_____	_____	_____	_____

> " Failing to plan is planning to fail. "
>
> — Anonymous

Many Internet sites provide information on the future and being proactive. Start at the following site, then keep exploring.

http://www.uniquorn.,simplenet.com/dfgb.htm

WORKSHOP WRAP-UP

- Big thinkers don't allow daily personal stressors to interfere with their problem-solving ability.
- Proaction, no action, or reaction are three approaches to problem solving.
- A proactive problem solver studies trends and tries to stay ahead of them.
- Taking advantage of trends requires risk.

When Ingrid sits down at her desk, her day is planned. She wants to begin on the stack of materials left from last week when she wrote the report on steel industry competition for Mr. Ramicheck. She was glad to turn the report over to him last night, and now she expects to get on with the rest of her work.

As she sits at her desk, Mr. Ramicheck hands her the report and describes changes he wants her to make. Some of the changes were items she suggested to him during the original brainstorming session. She thought, then, that he ignored her good ideas. She considered including the ideas in the report anyway, but decided against it. She wishes she had followed her instinct.

Now that she has turned the report in, she doesn't want to rewrite it. To change the report after it's written is just not a good idea.

Ingrid realizes that she also has some personal reasons for not wanting to rewrite the report. She can't finish the two priorities on her desk and get them out in time for her weekend ski trip if she does more work for Mr. Ramicheck. She's thinking about approaching him to argue her case about leaving the report as it is.

> There is nothing permanent except change.
>
> — Heraclitus

What's Inside

In these pages, you will learn to:

Expect Change

Change is the only constant in life. Looking at recent history, you can see great changes created by technology.

Fifty years ago, automation, for the most part, represented a vision for the future. America built almost everything by hand. Thirty years ago, typewriters were considered advanced technology. Fewer than five years ago, computers were produced with one gigabyte hard drives.

One of the greatest changes for you as an employee is the recent abundance of information that aids in decision making. With the touch of a few computer buttons, you can access financial reports and customer data bases, payroll data and tax forms, archived research and business letters—information that took days to locate in the past.

With the Internet, you can research any subject and expect to receive an instantaneous response.

For some, change makes daily events interesting, challenging, and stimulating; but for others, change represents frustration, fear, and disruption. Nowhere is this more apparent than at work where responsibilities, co-workers, supervisors, and rules change as economic and societal pressures shift. All of this change creates chaos for problem solvers who make their decisions based on current conditions and information.

As you complete daily tasks, expect change, and use it to your advantage. Here are some ways:

♦ Utilize changed conditions to create new or improved ideas.
♦ Eliminate irrelevant or outdated processes when change allows.
♦ Improve lines of communication by developing brainstorming or discussion groups to evaluate the changes.
♦ Reassign priorities to match the changed conditions.
♦ Reassign personnel for greater efficiency.

> "The world hates change, yet it is the only thing that has brought progress."
>
> — Charles F. Kettering

What's Changing?

What significant changes have occurred in your work, school, or social life within the last one, five, or ten years? Have you graduated, taken a job, married, relocated to another city, or received a promotion? In the chart below, write all the changes you remember. When you finish, place a check mark by the changes you believe affected your life the most then explain how the changes affected you.

Work changes

1. _____

_____

2. _____

_____

3. _____

_____

How the changes affected me: _____

_____

School changes

1. _____

_____

2. _____

_____

3. _____

_____

How the changes affected me: _____

_____

Personal changes

1. _____

_____

2._____

_____

3._____

_____

How the changes affected me: _____

_____

_____

Effect of Change on Problem Solving

The problem solving process would be easier if the problem you started with remained the same, but, often, that's not the case. The problem may change immediately, after you've formulated a plan, or after you've reached a decision. Consider the examples below.

- A restaurant manager develops a staffing schedule for cooks and waiters each week, then sees the schedule fall apart as employees call in sick or experience personal emergencies.
- An experienced administrative assistant who expects to spend the morning making decisions about how to handle an ever-growing stack of projects changes his direction when a supervisor hands over a proposal to be word processed by noon.
- The real estate agent who spends several hours deciding which house to show a prospective buyer learns after picking up the client that he has decided he wants a condominium instead of a house.

- A chemical company owner who spends two years studying locations, accessibility to transportation, and zoning laws before deciding on a new building site discovers that environmentalists object to her use of the land and plan a media campaign against the company's proposed location.
- The floral designer who takes an order by phone then creates a lovely arrangement gets a call from his customer requesting roses instead of tulips, which means the arrangement has to be taken apart.
- A veterinary assistant who decides on the order in which he will wash three dogs is asked to shampoo another dog first because the owner is waiting.

> Any change or reform you make is going to have consequence you don't like.
>
> — Mo Udall

Change Affects Work Decisions

You make decisions at work every day. Think of a problem you needed to solve in the last year and the changing conditions that influenced your problem solving process. State the problem below; then list the conditions that changed before you could solve the problem. Finish by identifying how the changing conditions affected you personally. An example is supplied.

The problem	Changing Conditions	Personal Effect
• *As a salesperson, I needed to reach my sales quota.*	*The warehouse was out of inventory on some items my customers wanted.*	*I had to convince customers to wait for back-ordered items or make a different choice.*
•		
•		
•		
•		
•		
•		

Making Change a Positive

Decisions aren't made in a vacuum. With all the decisions you'll ever make, you'll have to factor in change. How good you are at this will determine the degree of satisfaction or frustration in your work. You can do several things to make change serve you. Review the tips and the examples that follow.

1. **Think positively.** This is the old "glass half full, half empty" line of thought. If you consider change as good, you'll look at changing conditions as promising better solutions.

    You expect to take a day off on Friday and have worked diligently all week to get a project finished by Thursday afternoon. At 2 p.m. on Thursday, your supervisor tells you about a major change that will take at least six hours to incorporate into the plan. You decide to stay as long as needed on Thursday to finish the job, so you can take Friday off. This decision makes your supervisor happy, and you agree that the final project is better than the original.

2. **Be flexible.** If your personality leans toward structure and organization, that's good; but make sure you're not so inflexible that you overlook alternate solutions to problems.

    A client asks you for a layout design then changes his mind about what he wants. As a graphic artist, you fight for your original idea because you liked it and don't want to make the change, but also because you don't want to mess up the schedule you've established for this project. You finally explore other thinking because this is a loyal client. At the end you recognize that your new design is better than the first.

3. **Leave personal issues at home.** Your personal issues may be of primary importance to you, but a business cannot survive if it allows the personal concerns of its employees to hurt the company.

    Your children's dentist works 9 a.m.–5 p.m. Monday through Friday, which means you have to take time off from work each time either of them has an appointment. You don't want to change dentists because your children like this one. You finally decide to change dentists because personal issues are influencing your ability to get a promotion. You compete with co-workers who don't have the same problems.

> " The main dangers in life are the people who want to change everything or nothing. "
>
> — Lady Nancy Astor

4. **Use your creativity.** Take advantage of the opportunity to become creative if change allows.

A patient services employee regularly transports patients from their hospital rooms to the X-Ray department, physical therapy center, or laboratories. Due to construction in the halls, she detours several times trying to reach their destination. Patients become frustrated at the long route, so she develops a short dialogue about the changes and talks to the patients as they ride.

5. **Locate new information.** If changes make the current information unusable, look for other information. Don't get stuck in a rut because of a mismatch between the decision you need to make and the material you spent days or months gathering.

A data base management specialist spends several weeks comparing the data a company wants to gather about customers with the software programs that will capture this information. Prepared to go to the client with a recommendation, the specialist receives a phone call from the client, who requests a data base change. The software the specialist plans to recommend is no longer the right answer. The specialist decides to start over, looking for a program that will answer the client's needs.

6. **Fit square pegs into square holes.** Problem solving is about fitting the solution to the question or concern. If you have a great solution that's not right for the problem, you've wasted your time.

A news writer for a religious paper has an idea for an exposé on the town's leading employer and wants to convince her editor to run the story, but the paper she work for is targeted to family issues, not civic or political matters. She decides it would be inappropriate to pitch the story to the editor.

7. **Juggle the priorities.** Today's problem may be relegated to the back burner tomorrow when another problem becomes more important. You can't allow yourself to become so invested in a problem that's its significance is overrated.

A marketing assistant is asked to analyze the company's web site and make recommendations for improvements. She becomes so engrossed in the project that she resents her employer who assigns another problem with a greater priority.

> "That's the risk you take if you change: that people you've been involved with won't like the new you. But other people who do will come along."
>
> — Lisa Alther

8. **Accept change.** Fighting change leaves you frustrated and drained. Usually the change occurs anyway. Your health will be better, your relationships will improve, and your life will be happier if you accept what you cannot change.

A magazine editor is told by his publisher to develop a new design and freshen up the type style of the magazine. The editor, who created the current look, resists the idea and debates the value of the change with his employer. When he realizes his job is endangered, he designs the new look and adjusts to the changes over time.

ACTIVITY 6.3

Letting Change Serve You

Change serves some people well and discourages others. How well do you use change? Review the tips shown above for making change a positive experience than evaluate yourself as being an Excellent, Fair, or Poor user of change.

1.	Think positively. When I get lemons, I make lemonade.	Excellent	Fair	Poor
2.	Be flexible. Give me a change, and I'll take off in a different direction if necessary.	Excellent	Fair	Poor
3.	Leave personal issues at home. My supervisor never hears me whine or complain about how changes at work cause problems at my home.	Excellent	Fair	Poor
4.	Use your creativity. There's a part of me that loves being creative. Give me a problem and I'll find a creative solution.	Excellent	Fair	Poor
5.	Locate new information. Digging in and finding out what I need to know is part of my job. If I have a problem to solve, I'll throw out the unneeded information and start over.	Excellent	Fair	Poor
6.	Juggle the priorities. See all these balls I keep in the air? While I juggle, the balls change. I just keep on juggling.	Excellent	Fair	Poor
7.	Fit square pegs in square holes. I'm not wedded to a solution. If it doesn't match the problem, I'll find a solution.	Excellent	Fair	Poor
8.	Accept change. Here today, gone tomorrow is a phrase that doesn't bother me. Tell me a change is coming, and I'll prepare for it.	Excellent	Fair	Poor

Barriers to Change

Some change is expected—you see it coming. Some is unexpected—it comes out of nowhere. In today's rapidly advancing technological world, people often raise barriers to change because they're not prepared for it.

Resistance to change is often rooted in a lack of understanding. Examples can be found in every industry where many employees resist using computers because

they are untrained and, therefore, afraid of introducing a tool they are unable to control. The key for the employees is becoming trained.

Consider the barriers to change described below. Do any of these barriers affect your work?

1. **Losing the vision of the company.** Do you get so caught up in day-to-day details that you forget the vision? Stop every now and then and think about what the company does, why customers buy its products or services, and the path of growth the company has taken. Can you envision the future based on what you know about the past?

2. **Unwillingness to take a risk.** Risk keeps coming up as you read the workshops in this book. Are you willing to take the risks that come with change? Are you comfortable making decisions when the outcome is unclear?

3. **Inability to think critically.** Are you stuck in a mold where you can't see the possibilities in new ideas and better ways of doing things? Do you need to step back from routine and allow the creative part of your mind to engage?

4. **Focus on failures.** Mistakes are learning opportunities. If you remember only the failures, you'll never see the opportunities. Can you put the past behind you or use it to make a better future?

5. **Involving the personal.** Has your life changed since you assumed your present position? Are your personal goals still in keeping with the company's goals?

6. **Unwillingness to learn new things.** Is learning the same as living for you or is it something you tolerate when it's forced on you? You can't solve new problems with old ideas.

7. **Attitude that "change is no good."** If change wasn't good, your company wouldn't be growing, your job wouldn't exist, and your income would be in question. Do you always assume that change is bad, or do you see the good that can come from structured change?

> " Life belongs to the living and he who lives must be prepared for change. "
>
> — Johann Wolfgang won Goethe

Identify the Barriers

Barriers to creative problem solving exist in just about every job. Identify three problems you've solved recently and describe the barriers that kept you from doing your best work. In column 1, write the problem; then in column 2, write the number of the barrier that influenced your decision making from the list below. Add other barriers that you experienced. Describe how you got around each barrier.

Barriers to Problem Solving

1. Losing the vision of the company.

2. Unwillingness to take a risk.

3. Inability to think critically.

4. Focus on failures.

5. Involving the personal.

6. Unwillingness to learn new things.

7. Attitude that "change is no good"

Problem One   **Barriers I Experienced**

_____   _____

_____   _____

How I got around the barrier_____

_____

Problem Two   **Barriers I Experienced**

_____   _____

_____   _____

How I got around the barrier_____

_____

Problem Three   **Barriers I Experienced**

_____   _____

_____   _____

How I got around the barrier_____

_____

WORKSHOP WRAP-UP

- Change is here to stay.
- People put up barriers when they don't expect change.
- Change affects the decision making and problem solving processes..
- Being able to turn change into a positive can add satisfaction to your work.

7

ou've watched the cut back in management positions over the last year and a half; so it's no surprise when Eric, your supervisor, is reassigned to another office. The president of your company announces that a self-managed, decision-making team will operate your division. When you hear your name called at a staff meeting, you listen for the names of your team mates. "Sarah, Heather, Al, Antonio, you'll join Rick on the Green Team," the president says.

You've known your new team mates for years, but only to say hello in the hall or cafeteria. Now the team will make most of the decisions for your unit, including setting schedules, prioritizing work, monitoring production, and making recommendations for hiring and firing.

After a few weeks of awkwardness as the members get to know each other better, a routine appears. You are in charge of production because you get the most out of limited resources and time. Heather, who's

extremely organized, is in charge of receiving and shipping; Antonio handles quality control because he is a perfectionist; Sarah, a great negotiator, works with suppliers; and Al, an excellent communicator, handles personnel issues.

When the first team production reports arrive, they tell an interesting story. Production has gone up and defects have dropped since the team started making decisions. You're not surprised because the team members leave nothing to chance. Everyone realizes how important each person's team role is, so you respect and cooperate with each other to make big production gains.

As you reflect on the changes, you feel a sense of pride. Where you always depended on a supervisor before to tell you what to do, being responsible gives you a good feeling. When one person slips up, the others help out or give advice to keep production on track; and if one person scores a success, the entire team celebrates. Before it was just a job; now it's a job with a group of people who depend on you and upon whom you depend. It's a different way of working, but you decide you like it.

What's Inside

In these pages, you will learn to:

Why Teams?

Front-line workers often know more about the actual work that goes into delivering a product or service than supervisors, so common sense suggests that they should participate in making decisions and solving problems that occur during the handling of their day-to-day responsibilities. In the years of the industrial revolution, the United States built its economic success on factory production, and workers were paid to do, but not to think. In today's competitive information-based economy, the knowledge and talents of all workers are needed.

Decision-making teams have grown in popularity with both employers and employees as an outgrowth of this knowledge economy. A recent survey by the Massachusetts Institute of Technology found that 35 percent of all companies involve at least half their employees in some form of group decision making. When 4,500 workers were asked in another survey if they wanted more influence on work decisions, 65 percent said yes according to USA TODAY.

All members of a decision-making and problem-solving team share equally in the process and all are equally responsible for the outcome. This is similar to a sports team where each player is responsible for a position, and no one position is more important than the others. When one player drops the ball, the whole team suffers; if one person makes a great play, the whole team celebrates.

Companies establish decision-making teams for many different purposes. A sampling of purposes is shown in the list below. Perhaps you've participated in a team that can be added to the list of examples.

Purposes and Members of Typical Decision-Making Teams

Team Purpose	Typical Members
Development of a new line of products	Designers, marketers, production staff, representative from budget office
Annual holiday party	Representative from each department
New advertising campaign	Copywriters, artists, account executives, media staff
Relocation to another city	Human resources staff, departmental representatives, corporate officer
New logo	Graphic artist, public relations representative, departmental representatives

Advantages of Teams

Allowing team members to have a voice in how decisions are made provides four major advantages: (1) creative approaches to problem solving, (2) job satisfaction, (3) improved quality, and (4) increased performance.

Creative Approaches to Problem Solving. When team members know first-hand what is going on, they can see where problems and opportunities exist and can correct mistakes or try new ideas.

Job Satisfaction. The reward that comes from being responsible for the result makes team members feel important and motivates them to work harder and more efficiently at their jobs, which increases production.

Improved Quality. Responsibility for the final product creates the desire to deliver high quality.

Increased Performance. Reliance on other team members establishes relationships that reduce rancor, conflict, and lost time.

ACTIVITY 7.1

Name The Advantage

The success of the decision-making teams described below relates to one or more of the four major advantages of teams. Beside each description, write a 1, 2, 3, or 4 to identify the primary advantage.

1. Creative approaches to problem solving

2. Job satisfaction

3. Improved quality

4. Increased performance

Decision-Making Teams	Advantages
1. Since the production workers in a pottery factory were asked to sign their names on the bottom of each piece, pottery imperfections have reduced by 74 percent.	3
2. After a team of real estate agents was assigned to develop a new marketing plan for a three-year-old subdivision, sales increased by 19 percent.	
3. The rate of transfers and resignations in bakery personnel went from 24 percent to 6 percent after teams were assigned to bake certain types of pastries, such as wedding cakes, party favors, and breads for restaurants.	
4. When a team was assigned to operate a box manufacturing unit, new ways were developed to correct mistakes and production rose by 16 percent.	

Answers: 3, 4, 2, 1

Characteristics of Good Decision-Making Teams

A strong decision-making team exhibits twelve characteristics. If any one of these is missing, the team cannot perform at its highest level. Compare the characteristics listed below with the characteristics of teams you have served. Were all twelve characteristics present? If not, was your team successful?

Twelve Characteristics of Good Decision-Making Teams

1. Members exhibit an interest in doing well.
2. Each member believes in the team's vision.
3. Members share a team goal.
4. Leadership ability of some type is apparent in each member.
5. Team members possess common values.
6. Support and cooperation is present among members.
7. Each team member exhibits a sense of duty and responsibility.
8. Members desire challenge and opportunity.
9. A non-judgmental attitude exists.
10. The atmosphere is motivational.
11. The team looks at the big picture.
12. All members recognize the good work of other members.

> " Clearly, no group can create ideas as an entity. Only individuals can do this. A group of individuals may, however, stimulate one another in the creation of ideas. "
>
> — Estill L. Green

Your Team

You've probably served on a team of some type. Perhaps it was a work team, a sports team, an armed forces team, a team running or walking for charity, or some other group that came together to serve a single purpose. Identify the type of team and its purpose below, then describe what the team was able to do that you could not have done by yourself.

Type of team (*work, sports, charity, church, other*):

_____

Team purpose (*raise money for AIDS research, design a brochure, compete in sports*):

_____

What the team did that I could not have done by myself: _____

_____

_____

Team Leader's Role in Decision Making

Teams need leadership, even though they may not need supervision. Often a leader elected from within the team facilitates decision making by calling the team together, coordinating agendas, and following up on goals and results. Sometimes the leadership duties rotate between members on a regular basis to assure that no one individual dominates.

The team leader's job is to make sure that everyone on the team is heard and to create an atmosphere where ideas can be presented without fear of ridicule. Some ideas in their earliest stages appear useless, but with additional thought become great ideas. Unless a leader assures that these ideas are heard, they will drop away. When the idea for Mail Boxes Etc., a profitable packaging and shipping firm, was first presented, many thought it was silly to try to start a company to compete with the United States Postal Service. Today, Mail Boxes Etc. retail stores all over the country offer consumers an alternative to using their local post offices for mailing services.

> " Coming together is a beginning.
> Keeping together is progress.
> Working together is success. "
>
> — Henry Ford

Without a leader who establishes an environment of trust and objectivity that is fair and supportive of all members, the team can lose its group goal and inch toward individual achievement. Each team member has to be able to rely on all other team members to work for the good of the team, to put individual achievement aside, and to resist taking advantage of other members.

The leader should encourage people to do things differently and to try to find new and better ways of reaching the team's goal. Use the check list below to develop your skills as a team leader.

Team Leader's Checklist

✓ Call all members together.
✓ Assure that all members are heard.
✓ Establish and protect the trust among members.
✓ Introduce change.
✓ Encourage new ideas.

> Teamwork is the fuel that allows common people to attain uncommon results.
>
> — Anonymous

Trusting the Decisions

Every person on a team must be able to trust the decisions of other members. Usually, when we think of trust, we are considering the believability of an individual. Trust in decision-making teams is broader and can be divided into three categories: (1) trusting in goal agreement (2) trusting each member's knowledge, and (3) trusting each member's attitude.

Trusting in Goal Agreement

If any team member appears to disagree with the group's goal, his or her decision-making ability will be affected, most likely showing up as procrastination, argumentative behavior, or lowered enthusiasm. This creates distrust and dissension on the team. A team that doesn't agree on its goal will find itself engaged in petty confrontations that undermine the team's problem-solving ability.

Trusting Each Member's Knowledge

When a team engages in a physically dangerous task, it is clear to all that every member must be knowledgeable about his or her responsibility and must be able to apply the knowledge in a satisfactory manner. Imagine being a member of a precision flying team and distrusting the knowledge of another team member or being one of a fighting team in time of war. While few team assignments carry this level of risk, lack of trust in the knowledge of team mates is detrimental to any team's success. Consider these examples:

- A sales team member exhibits poor product knowledge.
- An accountant on a tax team does not keep up with annual IRS changes.
- An orchestra member practices infrequently.
- A member of a landscaping team is unable to identify plants.

Trusting Each Member's Attitude

Decisions are influenced by the attitude of team members. When all members demonstrate a "can-do, let's fix it" approach to a problem, the team can achieve great results. This is seen in fund-raising and membership drives where teams compete to raise the largest amount of money or sign the the greatest number of new members. Conversely, team performance decreases if team members are suspected of allowing personal motives to influence their decisions. Time schedules sometimes cause conflict because the personal preferences of team members conflict with team needs. Guard carefully against allowing your personal motives to enter into your decision-making process. This is one of the fastest routes to failure as a team member.

Removing Team Decision-Making Obstacles

Communication keeps team work alive. According to Price Pritchett in the book *Teamwork*, communication is the make-or-break issue in group problem solving. He says that second-rate communication is the kiss of death for high-quality teamwork. For each of the trust factors described on the preceding page, consider how good communication could break the log jam of mistrust.

Communication and Goal Agreement

When your team disagrees about the goal or the problem, speak frankly with the group. The team cannot make an appropriate decision or solve a problem if members don't reach agreement on the desired result. As a team member, it's your responsibility to bring the issue out into the open. Say to your teammates, "We don't seem to agree on our goal, and I'd like to talk about it now before it damages our team."

> Alone we can do so little; together we can do so much.
>
> — Helen Keller

Communication and Distrust of Knowledge

If you suspect a team mate is too inexperienced or untrained to participate fully on the assigned team, approach the team with a tactful but direct question, "Does everyone feel comfortable with his or her team responsibilities? If we're to solve this problem, we must assign ourselves to the tasks that use our talents. If any of us lacks the knowledge to do our best work, we need to change the assignments."

If you get a brush-off from the team or a response you disbelieve from individual members, continue to pursue the matter tactfully. Chances are that if you've noticed a weakness in a team assignment, others have also. By bringing the subject up, you will open the lines of communication.

Communication and Distrust of Attitude

Confronting a team member about a poor attitude may be one of the hardest things you'll ever do, but doing so is essential. When you experience a team slow down or aberrant team behavior, say to the group. "I believe the reason we are not able to make progress is because we don't all share the same attitude about working on this team. Let's get our differences out in the open so we can move on."

Purchase Order Dilemma

Read the case below; then describe why the team can't reach its goal. Offer a solution.

Case Study

The bookkeeper at a small construction company approached his supervisor and asked if a problem-solving team could be assigned to develop a better process for ordering equipment and supplies. The problem, he explained, was that he never knew how much money the company owed. "How can I budget when people order whatever they want and never tell me about it?"

Four people are assigned to the team and appear eager to assist.

❖ James, a long-timer with the company has ordered supplies for years without purchase orders. This is the only job he's ever had.

❖ Makela has been around for only six months. Before, she worked for a large national company that required purchase orders.

❖ T.R. is in marketing where he is well known for creating ad campaigns that bring in business. He's glad to help but hopes the team doesn't take too much of his time.

❖ The bookkeeper, Donald, wants the decision-making process to be handled well and expects to stay at the task until he's satisfied with the result.

After two weeks of meeting every other day, the nerves of team members are frayed and a purchase order process is nowhere in sight.

Possible reasons the team is not reaching its goal:

1. _____

2. _____

3. _____

4. _____

5. _____

My solutions:

1. _____

2. _____

3. _____

4. _____

5. _____

Problem Encountered by Teams

Team decision making is difficult; and, like any other group, work teams encounter problems. These pitfalls fit into several categories:

Teams Disagree. Teams are made up of independent thinkers; that is one of the advantages of putting bright people together to solve problems. It's natural that members will disagree. When the disagreement leads to objective debate, it helps the team focus on the goal. Debate is bad only when it becomes personal, critical, or unfocused, causing team members to lose confidence and trust in each other and in the team process.

Think how citizens of the United States elect senators to serve as a team of lawmakers in Washington, D.C. The senators sometimes agree, but often they don't. If you watch the news, you know that senators like to talk about how they disagree in order to distinguish themselves as independent thinkers with the people back home. They are, however, still a team; and in times of national crisis or important decision making, they come together to try to reach the best decisions for all citizens.

Group Thinking. One danger for teams is that members fall into a mode of "group thinking" because no one wants to speak out about what they think. When team members become personally involved, they refrain from hurting feelings, speaking an opposing view, or creating conflict. Group thinking can be deadly for the decision-making process because it reduces the number of innovative ideas.

With group think, the discussion often ends before all members get a chance to be heard. Since some members take longer than others to create their ideas and get them out, their input never has a chance to be considered.

All Talk And No Action. Reaching agreement may be easier than following through. The problem-solving process is incomplete until the decision is implemented and action is taken.

Failure to Use Outside Resources. All problems cannot be solved by team members, but it's easy for the team to fall into a trap of looking only to themselves for answers. Key individuals and resources outside the team hold information that often is needed before a decision can be made. Examine the decision-making process of your teams to identify resources that can add clarity and information.

Failure to Communicate. Team members get to know each other well, but they cannot read minds. Failing to speak what you're thinking, inability to outline your points in a clear, precise manner, and failing to listening contribute to the problems within many teams. If you experience trouble getting your viewpoint across, evaluate your communication skills and make notes before team meetings, so you can make your position clear.

> " The strength of the team is each individual member...the strength of each individual member is the team. "
>
> — Phil Jackson
> Coach of the Chicago Bulls

Evaluate Your Team Skills

What talents do you bring to a team? Are you a good listener, an excellent speaker, a strong leader, a can-do personality? Read the team goal below and list the talents and skills you offer to the team.

My Team

You've been chosen to serve on a team of four to purchase framed pictures, wall hangings, and other decorations for your company's new offices.

The talents and skills I bring to this team:

1. _____   _____

2. _____   _____

3. _____   _____

4. _____   _____

5. _____   _____

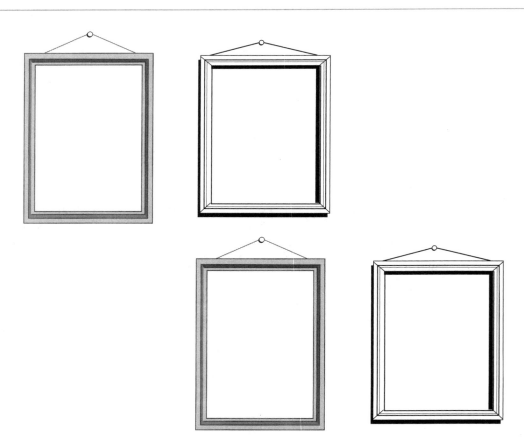

Examine Your Job

In your current job or a job you wish to pursue, specific duties might be handled better by a decision-making team than by an individual. Take a minute to think about some of these duties. Which one could be handled better by a team? Complete the chart below with ideas from your job.

My job: _____

Responsibilities That Could Be Handled Better By a Team

1. _____

2. _____

3. _____

4. _____

5. _____

How Team Work Would Help

_____
_____

_____
_____

_____
_____

_____
_____

_____
_____

> If I could solve all the problems myself, I would.
>
> — Thomas Edison
> On why he had a team of 21 assistants

Creating A Team Decision-Making Plan

Decision-making teams need a plan so that all the important elements of the goal are covered and agreed on. A plan is a simple, direct outline that describes the team's purpose and responsibilities. Five questions are answered in a team plan:

1. What is to be done (the goal)?

2. Why is this goal important?

3. To whom is the team accountable?

4. What team risks or dangers may the members encounter (examples: lack of support from management, jealousy from other employees)

5. How can the team eliminate risks and dangers?

By using the team planning form below, you can answer these questions before any work is done by the team. Doing so eliminates the risk that the team will solve the wrong problem or answer an incorrect question.

> " I think any player will tell you that individual accomplishments help your ego, but if you don't win, it makes for a very, very long season. It counts more that the team has played well. "
>
> — David Robinson

Team Planning Form

Name of Company:_____

What the company does: _____

What the team does: _____

To whom the team is accountable:_____

Risks or dangers this team may encounter:_____

Ways to eliminate the risks or dangers to the team:_____

_____

_____

_____

GETTING CONNECTED

For team decision-making exercises, log on to the Internet and go to the Web site shown below. For additional team information, use a search engine and search for the word team work.

http://www.mideca.org/tdm.htm

WORKSHOP WRAP-UP

- Front-line workers often know more than a supervisor about the actual work.
- All team members share equally in what happens.
- A strong decision-making team exhibits specific characteristics.
- The team leader makes sure everyone on a team is heard.
- Each person on a team must be able to trust the decisions of other members.
- Members must be able to apply knowledge in a satisfactory manner.
- Communication keeps team work alive.
- Each team should have a decision-making plan.

The district manager walks in, shakes Ramon's hand, and says, "Congratulations, Ramon, you're moving up to replace Carol as manager of human resources when he retires." Ramon is pleased and takes a moment to reflect on the last three years as Carol's assistant.

Carol is a good mentor. He allows employees to make decisions as if they were in charge. However, every big decision requires his final approval before it's implemented.

Now, it is Ramon's turn. As manager, he will have final decision-making authority over 15 departmental employees and human resources policy-making responsibility for the five company locations. He's looking forward to the challenge.

Ramon's first day as manager is uneventful; but on the second day, one of the assistants brings him a stack of recommendations for salary increases company wide. Before, as Carol's assistant, Ramon gathered information and submitted reports regarding raises, but he didn't have to sign his name and be held accountable for the results.

Signing his name to the documents makes him think carefully about making decisions that will cost the company money. The raises alone will account for $250,000 in the first year. Do all these people deserve raises? Are the recommended amounts equitable? Ramon is struck by the importance of his position and recognizes the decision will have a large impact. People depend on him to make the right decision and to face up to it when he's questioned. For a moment only, he wishes Carol were present to consult.

Ramon's excitement increases as he realizes it is time to take charge. He signs the forms and puts them in his out basket, knowing full well that he will stand by his decisions if employees complain that the raises are too low or management suggests they are too high.

What's Inside

In these pages, you will learn to:

> Discovery consists of seeing what everybody has seen and thinking what nobody has thought.
>
> — Albert von Szent-Gyorgyi

What Is Accountability?

Being accountable means you are responsible for your choices and their results. You take ownership, accept blame, or enjoy the reward for each decision. You don't make excuses, or disappear when your mistake is discovered.

Accountability exists in every job, from entry-level employee to chief executive officer. To accept accountability easily, you need self-esteem, confidence, and courage. It may be embarrassing to say, "I misjudged,"or "I made a mistake," but sometimes you must do so. Here are a few other statements you'll hear from people who hold themselves accountable. Practice using some of these when you want to show accountability.

"That was my fault."
"You're right."
"Blame me."
"I'm responsible."
"I'm sorry."
"Please accept my apology."
"I should have taken your advice."
"I caused the problem. I'll fix it."

Ramon realized that his accountability increased as his responsibilities in the organization grew. He was prepared and ready to accept ownership of his decisions.

Look at the list and compare the behaviors of workers who accept accountability and who do not accept accountability.

Accountable Behaviors	Unaccountable Behaviors
Accepts responsibility	Blames others
Steps forward	Fades away
Admits a mistake	Covers up
Confronts the problem	Hides the problem
Deals with failure	Makes excuses
Fixes what is wrong	Passes the correction to others
Owns both good and bad results	Disowns poor results

> I was gratified to be able to answer promptly. I said, 'I don't know.'
>
> — Mark Twain

Wendy's Accountability

Review the case study and describe what Wendy should do to make herself accountable.

Case Study

As the manager of an automobile body shop, Wendy checks all car repairs before they leave the building. When a customer brings her car back the first time because she is dissatisfied with the paint match on her hood, Wendy cheerfully orders a repaint. After the customer returns a second time and complains about small bubbles in the repaint, Wendy calculates how much money the shop will lose in labor and supplies because of this picky customer, then decides how to respond to her request for another repaint.

1. What are Wendy's choices?_____

_____

2. What will be the result of each choice? _____

_____

3. What should Wendy do?_____

_____

Responsibility and Accountability

Responsibility and accountability are similar but distinguishable terms. What is the difference? The level of responsibility determines an employee's amount of accountability; however all workers are 100% accountable for their assigned responsibilities. The president of an art museum, for example, may be responsible for a multi-million dollar budget, so his level of accountability is greater than that of a department head who is responsible for a $100,000 budget. An account executive with a large client has greater responsibility than the receptionist whose client contact is minimal.

Responsibility starts when you take on a duty. With the duty comes accountability for performance. A bookkeeper for a charity assumes a duty to manage the books and is held accountable for all dollars received and spent.

> " I am responsible. Although I may not be able to prevent the worst from happening, I am responsible for my attitude toward the inevitable misfortunes that darken life. Bad things do happen; how I respond to them defines my character and the quality of my life. I can choose to sit in perpetual sadness immobilized by the gravity of my loss, or I can choose to rise from the pain and treasure the most precious gift I have—life itself. "
>
> — Walter Anderson

Making Yourself Accountable

Accountability is not something to be avoided. You cannot be successful in your career, nor in life, without taking responsibility. In some careers, making decisions and being accountable is the biggest part of the job. For example, a quality control specialist's entire job is to examine and approve goods leaving a plant, and a physician's primary responsibility is to diagnose illnesses and make decisions about patient care. Both of these workers must be accountable for their good and bad choices.

Your decisions affect many people, and it is to them that you are accountable. Some will agree with you, and others will not. The way you respond is a measure of who you are as a person. In the case of the quality control specialist, the worst outcome will be an unhappy customer; however, a physician who makes an incorrect choice may be responsible and accountable for a patient's death.

We are all accountable to someone. When you solve work-related problems, you are accountable to your boss; your boss is accountable to the CEO; the CEO is accountable to the stockholders or the owner. Ultimately, the corporation is accountable to society and customers. As an employee, you made a decision to be at your job on time and to do your best work. Your company made a decision to be in business and to provide a product or service to society. As an employee of the organization, in a sense you are responsible also to the public and to society.

> **It is always better to under promise and over produce.**
>
> — Anonymous

Hold Me Accountable

A list of workers and the people to whom they are accountable is shown below. Think about the organizations or people with whom you associate and add other types of workers and the people to whom they are accountable.

Worker	People To Whom Workers Are Accountable
Bus driver	passengers, employer, pedestrians
Teacher	students, parents, school board
Mail carrier	recipient and sender of mail, U.S. Government
Conference speaker	audience, selection committee, sponsoring organization
Pest control specialist	building owner, employer, users of the environment
Hotel clerk	guests, corporation
Chemical plant owner	employees, neighboring residents, society

_____   _____

_____   _____

_____   _____

_____   _____

_____   _____

Several questions will help you decide your measure of accountability regarding any decision. When facing any major responsibility, ask yourself the questions shown below.

♦ Who is impacted by my decision?
♦ Does the decision affect people outside my company?
♦ How will my decision affect all people and organizations impacted?
♦ How will I be held accountable?
♦ Do I want to take the responsibility?

> It is my firm belief that I have a link with the past and a responsibility to the future. I cannot give up; I cannot despair. There's a whole future, generations to come. I have to keep trying.
>
> — Hussein, King of Jordan

Take Ownership

Think back and remember a decision you made recently that didn't get the result you wanted.

Describe the decision, who was impacted, the effect of the decision, what went wrong, and how you took ownership.

My decision:_____

_____

Who was impacted:_____

_____

What went wrong:_____

_____

The effect: _____

_____

How I took ownership: _____

_____

Team Accountability

Teams share accountability, with each member being accountable to both the company and teammates. The type of accountability to the company comes from the team's purpose, and accountability to members is determined by the task to which the team member is assigned. When team members fail to assume responsibility and accountability, team spirit is destroyed and the team's ability to reach its goal is reduced. If you are a team member, you are accountable for handling your tasks promptly, accurately, and appropriately.

> The willingness to accept responsibility for one's own life is the source from which self-respect springs.
>
> — Joan Didion

GETTING CONNECTED

The Internet has many sites to help organizations gauge their accountability. Try searching for the key terms: accountability in decision making or worker accountability. To get started, log on to the Web site shown below:

http://kapis.www.wkap.nl/kaphtml.htm/jrnlhome

WORKSHOP WRAP-UP

- Accountability means you are responsible for your choices and their results.
- All workers are accountable to someone.
- The level of responsibility determines the amount of accountability.
- You cannot be successful in work or life without being accountable.
- Teams are accountable to the company and to coworkers.

Checklist for Decision Making and Problem Solving

✓ Combining decision making and problem solving with critical thinking leads to great ideas and inventions.

✓ Making good decisions takes courage, determination, and confidence.

✓ Know that decisions are means, not ends.

✓ Match each problem with the appropriate decision-making technique.

✓ Be aware of personal characteristics that influence your decision-making.

✓ Identifying the real problem is the biggest decision-making challenge.

✓ Learning to think critically is like learning to read, write or become an engineer.

✓ Becoming an innovative problem solver requires taking risks.

✓ Sharing ideas with others in a group is a way for risk-adverse individuals to get their ideas discussed.

✓ Jump on an idea when it occurs.

✓ Breaking a problem down and locating connections or new associations among seemingly unrelated ideas is the central point in critical thinking.

✓ Asking questions, making checklists, brainstorming, imitating and debating are techniques to develop critical thinking skills.

✓ To make any decision, you need information.

✓ Seeing a problem in action is the best way to get information or to collect data.

✓ Using graphics, such as a T-chart, helps to illustrate alternatives in a decision- making process.

✓ Keeping track of the many pieces of information that go into a decision and evaluating each against a criteria is the purpose of a Decision Value Chart.

✓ Implementing the decision is the final step in the decision-making process.

✓ Develop two or three good solutions, then choose the one you think is best in the situation.

✓ Track your solution and evaluate whether your correctly solved the problem.

✓ Being able to place current activities and events in the context of a bigger picture makes you a more effective problem solver and therefore, more valuable to your employer.

✓ Seeing the big picture allows you to take actions to prevent or delay problems.

✓ Recognizing clues that allow you to see the big picture and predict the future is a skill.

✓ Studying trends and staying ahead of them are characteristics of proactive problem solvers.

Checklist for Decision Making and Problem Solving

✓ Expect change - it is the only constant in life.

✓ Thinking positively, being flexible, leaving personal issues at home, using your creativity, locating new information, fitting square pegs into square holes, and juggling priorities are strategies to make change serve you.

✓ Accept change.

✓ Fighting change only leaves you frustrated and drained.

✓ Don't let barriers to change affect your work

✓ Taking ownership means accepting blame and enjoying the reward for each decision.

✓ Recognizing that accountability exists in every job is key to your success.

✓ Accepting the accountability that comes with responsibility takes courage.

✓ Determining your level of accountability requires information.

✓ Sharing team accountability is essential.

Also in the
QUICK SKILLS SERIES

Attitude and Self-Esteem

Listening

Reading in the Workplace

Self-Management and Goal Setting

Speaking and Presenting

Writing in the Workplace

For information on new titles:
call 1-800-354-9706
or visit us on-line at
academic.cengage.com